NEWSPEAK

The Language of
Soviet Communism

NEWSPEAK

The Language of
Soviet Communism

(La langue de bois)

Françoise Thom

translated by Ken Connelly

The Claridge Press
London and Lexington

First published in French by Julliard, 1987

First published in Great Britain 1989

by The Claridge Press
43 Queen's Gardens
London W2
and Box 420
Lexington
Georgia 30648

P
119.3
T5613
1989

Typeset by
Wordsmiths Typesetting Ltd
London N1
and printed by
Short Run Press
Exeter, Devon

ISBN 1-870626-70-2

Thom, Françoise
Newspeak (La Langue de Bois)

1. Sociology 2. Philosophy 3. Linguistics

To Alain Besançon

CONTENTS

V THE HISTORY OF NEWSPEAK

Acknowledgement

I am very grateful to Charles Janson and Roger Scruton for their advice in the translation of this work, and for numerous stylistic suggestions.

London, April 1989   Ken Connelly

PREFACE TO THE ENGLISH EDITION

Many Westerners regard Gorbachev as the liquidator of communist ideology; as 'Soviet Dissident No 1', to use the striking expression of Andrei Sinyavsky. For them *langue de bois* has become a phenomenon of the past, an object of purely historical interest.

It is indeed the case that Gorbachev likes to emphasise that 'the global interests of humanity' come before those of the proletariat, or rather that the two cannot be separated. In this one almost seems to see a downright rejection of Leninism. Is Mikhail Gorbachev the grave-digger of communist ideology? In order to give a proper answer to this question one has to go beyond Gorbachev's sensational statements and pay due attention to what he writes and what he says in his speeches. For Leninism is not only a body of doctrines, which, thanks to the dialectic, can usually be revoked when expediency demands. Above all it is a style, to the analysis of which this book is devoted. Even a superficial examination of the works of the General Secretary shows in fact that Newspeak is intact, and that we are still dealing with a captive way of thinking propelled and programmed by Leninism. The word *'perestroika'* itself, the banner-word of Gorbachev's government, is undergoing the fate of all terms manipulated by Newspeak. It has come to mean so many things (beginning as 'the strengthening of work-discipline' and 'the struggle against corruption' and becoming in due course a synonym for '*glasnost*' and 'democratisation') that it can be exactly translated only as 'the Party line'.

Recent events in the Soviet Union show the extraordinary grip which Newspeak has on Soviet minds. At the very moment when the rulers are admitting to the regime's fiasco, it is Newspeak which dictates their remedies, inventing the disastrous slogan of 'acceleration', and setting the objective of 'democratisation', in place of democracy *tout court*. It is Newspeak which talks of 'improving the quality of Soviet laws'; of 'giving prices an economic foundation'; of 'making a more efficacious use of power'; of 'reinforcing the political methods of government'; of 'activating the human factor', of 'perfecting the relationship between the nationalities'; and so on. It is events alone that have the role of demonstrating that these formulae are absurd, whereas in a world free from Newspeak it would be human beings who would take the lead, by protesting against all such affronts to common sense and so forestalling the ruinous cost of leaving the events to disprove the formulae. *Glasnost* does allow the recognition of failure, but is helpless in face of people who formulate and seek to apply irrational policies. For *glasnost* does not attack Newspeak itself.

The Soviet Union can never embark on genuine reforms until it 'refuses the lie': not merely the lie about the past, but those about the present and the future. This means saying 'the Communist Party' instead of 'bureaucracy'; 'the socialist system' instead of 'the administrative command-system'; 'communist terror' instead of 'the infringement of Leninist norms'. In other words genuine reform requires a victory over Newspeak itself.

INTRODUCTION

The Soviet linguist N.J. Marr prophesied that the victorious proletariat would eventually free itself from the bonds of spoken language, subject as it was to humiliating natural constraints. Under Communism the workers would give up speech – the formal and reactionary medium bequeathed to them by the obscurantist past – and communicate directly, by pure thought alone.

However, it now seems that the rule of language, like that of the State, has been reinforced 'dialectically' under socialism, until the day of universal 'mutism' can dawn. For no other regime is as wordy as Communism, or as jealous of its monopoly of the word. No other regime knows better how to take control of language and use it for its own ends.

But the language it uses is not like everyday language. One can make out the usual words and expressions, but there is something quite foreign about it all; and its words and phrases cannot be described in the usual way. The lack of real content strikes one immediately. Until *glasnost*, the Soviet press carried almost nothing in the way of references to current events, few descriptions of real life, and very little information. The flood of words seems to spring from nowhere and yet it spreads daily into millions of printed texts, into radio and television. It seems able to keep pouring for ever and ever. But lack of content is not the

only distinctive thing about Soviet style: the language itself
seems to have undergone a mutation. For a long time now,
communist language has been recognized as a special
jargon. The Russians themselves call it 'wooden language'
(*dubovy yazyk* – literally, 'language of oak'), alluding to the
original ponderous administrative style favoured by the
Tsarist bureaucracy. In the 1920's people made fun of this
new language which was spreading throughout the press.
The satirical writer Milchail Zoschenko called it 'monkeys'
chatter': the Poles of the 'twenties referred to it as
congealed or 'ossified language'. Orwell was the first to
recognize that it was not just another jargon like the rest –
not something laughable and, in the last analysis, harmless –
but language itself, metamorphosed by ideology. He had an
insight into the role which Newspeak plays in the functioning of the totalitarian state.

The expression *langue de bois* (wooden language) has
passed into the French language: it describes any politicized
idiom or style marred by jargon. Because it is used loosely,
people forget that the phrase properly applies to a very
specific and precisely determined phenomenon. For
although the communist language has to fill all sorts of
newspapers, magazines and books eloquently and to nour-
ish innumerable speeches, it is perfectly uniform in structure. At the same time, the formal characteristics of
Newspeak[1] – syntactical, lexicographical and stylistic –
reveal its specific nature without fully accounting for it.
Newspeak's relation to reality differs utterly from that of
ordinary language. It parades itself as a scientific language
from which everything subjective has been excluded. It
claims to have a monopoly of truth. Yet that which it
describes does not actually exist; and that which does exist
in real life, Newspeak constantly represses beneath its
invocation of what *ought* to be. Newspeak is nothing but a
series of magical incantations, disguised as a chain of
self-evident axioms.

The peculiar strangeness of this language is due to the fact that, unlike other languages, it serves only one function: to be a vehicle for ideology[2]. It is thus immensurably less complex than ordinary language. In what follows I will demonstrate this lack of complexity, the crude devices which form the mechanics of Newspeak, and the uniform manner in which this language is constructed. Such is the purpose of this work[3].

I

NEWSPEAK DESCRIBED

"How have we changed the Russian language? ... a great many old words are no longer part of its vocabulary: the semantic meaning of a great many others has been changed: we have improved the grammatical structure of the language."

J. Stalin

"Clearly, people capable of using such phrases have ceased to remember that words have meanings."

G.Orwell

The first characteristic of Newspeak is that it has two modes: overt and covert. The overt mode – the language of editorials and official statements – exhibits a number of grammatical, lexical and stylistic features, which must be defined before we undertake any analysis of the whole system. This section does not give an exhaustive account of Newspeak: but it will suffice to show that Newspeak is easy to identify by its more striking characteristics, however hard it may be to define it. Many examples of Soviet and French Communist style will be given in order to give the reader a feel for Newspeak that will be as instinctive and infallible as that of a reader of *Pravda*.

SYNTAX

One can recognise a Newspeak text at a glance, without even bothering about what it means. It will have an unmistakable heaviness. The heaviness derives from the syntax and from certain mannerisms, like nervous tics, which almost persuade the reader that he is dealing with a parody of some other text. These characteristics can be summarised as follows:

Nominalization

Subordinate phrases using verbs or adverbs are replaced by nouns preceded by a preposition:

> In the nineteenth century, *as a decision and an elucidation* of the political conditions which had previously existed, the active mass of humanity divided itself into two groups: conservatives and revolutionaries.[4]

> It is *by means of the development of widespread activity* among the masses and with their support that conditions will be created *for the elaboration* ... of a Common Programme of government.[5]

> *After the elaboration* of the programme of supplies and *of the implementation* of the plans, it is vital to give the greatest

importance *to the amelioration* of the economic mechanism.

After the establishment of the balance sheets, the organisations within the Party and the unions must *make an objective
appreciation of* the contribution made by each collective.

Nominal syntagms such as these also replace relative
clauses and participles. Moreover, very often a *phrase*
containing a noun and a verb replaces a simple verb, so that
the verb is in some way given an auxiliary function. Thus 'to
express' becomes 'to find its expression', and 'to reflect'
becomes 'to find its reflection'. 'To take the decision to
cease fire' is regarded as much more stylish than 'to decide
to cease fire', and 'render aid' is always preferred to 'help'.
In all those examples the verb is somehow sacrificed to
the noun. Not all verbs, however, are similarly belittled.
Those which refer to *continuing processes* stand up better
against the pushing noun. The verbs which are liquidated
tend to be those which introduce the concept of time, and
especially the idea of temporal sequence, into a sentence:
for such verbs compel precision. 'Most verbs express what is
true, while nouns are ... the haven of empty forms,'[6] wrote
Valéry. Whenever possible, Newspeak avoids the precision
of the verb and opts for a vague timelessness, carefully
evading narrative while stressing the *movement* that is
immanent in all things. Newspeak retreats at the same time
from 'enunciation';[7] that is, from any identification of the
time when the statement is made, of the circumstances of
making it, or of the speaker responsible. This motive
accounts for another characteristic of Communist language:

The lack of shifters

According to Benveniste, "'shifters' are a group of 'empty' signs which do not refer to anything specific in the 'real world', but are 'filled' as soon as they are used by a speaker". These words change their sense with their content or with the circumstances of the speaker; hence their meaning 'cannot be understood without reference to the message'.[8]

Adverbs of time or place are often used as shifters: Newspeak uses them, however, as though their signification were invariable. 'Now' means 'in our period of time' (not 'the moment at which I am speaking'); 'tomorrow' means 'in the future' (not a day of the week). But it is the first and second person pronouns which are the predominant shifters; and it is interesting to see how they are used in Newspeak.

The pronoun 'I' has virtually disappeared, except in particularly solemn pronouncements: the second person pronoun is never used. On the other hand, 'we' crops up now and then, and always with the same meaning: the union of the people, the Party and the government. 'We' in Newspeak is never used indexically: its function, implicitly or explicitly, is to stand in opposition to the pronoun 'they' which refers negatively to the forces of reaction – each is the mirror-image of the other. 'We' represents in fact a third person with a positive connotation. In ordinary language, by contrast, the third person cannot (according to Benveniste) be put on a par with the first and second; rather, 'it is the impersonal form of the inflection of the verb'. Its referent is to the 'non-person' – 'the one who is absent', as the Arabian grammarians put it. In other words, terms like 'he' function, not as shifters, but as bound variables.

All these peculiarities point in the same direction: the target is the category of the individual who is to be eliminated.

Passive and impersonal phrases

One must refer here to Soviet literature since a great constructive advance *has been made* along that road.[9]

The mutual link between different theories and different sciences *has been strengthened* on the basis of cybernetics. This has stimulated discussion about the contribution of cybernetics to the scientific view of the world.

Wishes were expressed for augmentation of the pace of the improvement of trade.

Particularly close attention was given to the plans and prospects for commercial-economic cooperation.

Stress is put always on the process, and precise indications of time are rare. From this yet another characteristic of Newspeak follows:

Comparatives

Sentences like the following are commonplace:

The politics of the power of monopolies can give rise only to *more profound, more extensive contradictions*.[10]

The intensification of the crisis of monopoly-capitalism in France and the lessons of the great popular movement of May/June 1968 have given *yet greater depth* to that belief.[11]

This aspect of the analysis of Marxist-Leninist teaching has an *increasingly important* place in the documents of the Communist Party of the Soviet Union, and the activities of its leaders.

Under the conditions of mature socialism the bond between economic progress and socio-political and spiritual progress becomes *ever more close.*

When a conflict is mentioned, it's certain to be 'ever sharper' – a fact which always becomes 'increasingly clear'. Newspeak is full of these tirades and processes which, true to their nature, grow always more intense. This feature reminds one of bad essays written by pupils short of inspiration. One notices that the comparatives always lack their second term: 'more ...' – but more than what? Here again Newspeak spurns precision and sticks to abstractions. However, stress laid on the successions of phenomena appears difficult to reconcile with another characteristic of Newspeak:

The imperative mode

Every linguistic device for indicating *command* or *exhortation* is called upon, ranging from the imperative via the infinitive to the adverb:

The most important changes in Soviet society *must* receive profound scientific expression.

It is essential to try especially hard to give the necessary orientation to the social activity of the masses; the one which corresponds to the needs of social progress.

In every sphere of activity the proposals in the programme *must be* such as would foster the participation of the masses and the development of the working-class struggle ...[12]

Friendship *must* be intensified!

The combination of impersonal style with voluntarist discourse is typical of Newspeak; nowhere else, indeed, do we find such an oscillation between scientific objectivity and the peremptory barking of slogans.

All these characteristics can be found separately in the various jargons used by modern society. Scientific style is marred by the excessive use of nouns; bureaucratic jargon by its impersonality. The mania or comparatives frequently disfigures the writings of schoolteachers and journalists. But no other jargon simultaneously contains *all* the traits described in this chapter. Only Communist Newspeak combines these monstrosities, and it is precisely this that makes it unique and original.

Newspeak owes nothing to the other jargons of the contemporary world. On the other hand, Marxist-Leninist diction can be compared to the language of the Third Reich, which showed similar features – the same emphasis on processes, the same exhortatory rage – though to a lesser degree.

Communist diction gives itself away perhaps as much by its grammar as by its vocabulary. Its 'wooden' syntax has the same effect on languages as different as French, Russian, English and Chinese.

VOCABULARY

The Third Reich created only a tiny number of words in its glossary ... But it did change the value and frequency of words ... It seized for the Party what formerly belonged to everybody, it injected words with its own poison, and groups of words and the shape of phrases; it subjected all language to its terrible system ...

Victor Klemperer.

The vocabulary of Newspeak is not unfamiliar to the speaker of ordinary language. It refers to such things as peace, progress and cooperation. Yet the way these terms are used is always misleading. For the words deployed by Newspeak do not draw their meaning from contact with reality (not even the distorted reality of lies). Instead they relate to a prior system of ready-made interpretations; they rest, in other words, not on reality itself, but on a fixed commentary on reality. It is this canonical system which must be deciphered, since it is the real frame of reference: beside it the particular circumstances which give rise to speech are of little relevance. A study of the vocabulary of Newspeak reveals the fictitious movements and imaginary antagonisms which provide its dynamic, and which insulate it from the mischievous contingencies of the actual world of perception.

Newspeak possesses only a poverty-stricken vocabulary[13]: one can soon tour round it. It is enough to refer to a small number of key ideas of emotive analogies borrowed from elsewhere and diverted to the specific aims of the new language, on account of their powerful attraction for the mind, and of their versatility. The vocabulary of Newspeak is divided between the spheres of influence of these key ideas and the latent analogies.

Manicheism

The first and most important of these boss-ideas is that of a world deeply divided into two hostile and irreconcilable camps. This Manichean vision is an inexhaustible source of metaphors and commonplaces. For it introduces a basic dualism, around which most of the words belonging to the vocabulary may be organized. The vision is also a launching-pad for communist rhetoric.

This explains why so many terms in the vocabulary of Newspeak are taken from the military glossary.[14] The imagery of war is extended into areas which everyone has hitherto regarded as entirely bucolic. Where nothing more dramatic than the milking of cows or the digging of potatoes is happening we hear only of fronts, battles, attacks, resistance, captures of positions, strategies, and tactics. Peace itself becomes the object of a bitter struggle. Reading the communist press one gets the impression of a society perpetually in arms. The same taste for military terminology is to be found in the Nazi glossary, where the words *Kampf* (*kämpferisch*) and *marschieren* occur over and over again.[15]

The basic dualism has another effect that is no less important. No word in Newspeak is innocent; all are pre-interpreted. Some words relate only to the evil world which is doomed by history to destruction; others are the property of the forces of the future. Every concept belongs to one or other of the two camps – or rather, each concept is defined by its contrary, which lies on the opposite side of the divide between Communism and the enemy. Representatives of the socialist camp are thus champions of peace to the extent that their adversaries are warmongers. The fictitious enemy embodies every negative principle: as imperialist, he oppresses nations; as militarist he jeopardizes peace, etc.[16] The same concept is expressed in different words according to whether it is placed in the context of imperialism or of the liberated world of socialism. For example: *razvedchik* denotes an heroic Soviet agent; *shpion* indicates – and condemns – a foreign spy. Even more striking, the phrase *zavoyevanie kosmosa* (the conquest of space), used in connection with the Americans, is replaced by *osvoyenie kosmosa* (the benign development of space) when the USSR is referred to. Even space takes sides.

The particular function of the adjective Newspeak is to 'place' words in accordance with the immanent scheme of values. If by chance a neutral term appears, an adjective must be placed beside it, so as to push it into one camp or the other. So the key word 'forces' is never used by itself: 'forces' will be either 'progressive'; or 'reactionary'. According to Voltaire, the adjective is the great enemy of the noun. Nothing truer could be said about the adjective in Newspeak, whose role is precisely to volatilise the accompanying noun. Consider these examples, which show how the label destroys the contents, the noun's meaning being abolished by the value injected by the adjective: 'Kolkhozian opulence', 'revolutionary legality' and, under Gorbechev, 'socialist initiative' and 'socialist market'.[17]

Just as with space, time is made into either good or bad, useful or harmful. 'The old' is always opposed to 'the new' –

everything 'old' being disqualified as exploitatory while 'the new' promises mankind's universal liberation.

Unfortunately, however, matters are more complicated. The past contained some positive elements, the seeds of the future. Even in imperialist nations, progressive forces are at work as the working class carries on the struggle for liberation. On the other hand, the socialist world is not entirely free from reactionary or mercenary capitalist elements: these left-overs prevent an unbridled development of the collective economy.

The same struggle takes place therefore in three areas: between the two blocs, within the dimension in time, and within each camp; whence the importance of recognizing one's friends and unmasking one's enemies. In any given situation it is necessary to make the distinction, which is precisely the function of Newspeak armed by its vocabulary. Words are no longer used for their meanings but simply as tools in the process of selection. A system of co-ordinates, implicit or explicit, fixes the position of discourse. In this language, which claims to be so 'concrete', every device is used to convey what are in fact value-judgments. The forces of progress are always marching into the future. The standard of living 'rises' but that does not prevent the Party from planning increasingly 'large' programmes. Phrases like the following are typical:

> The new programme which was worked out after the Congress, for the eleventh five-year plan and the '80's, is even larger and is designed to continue the improvement of the people's well-being while bringing about a betterment of every aspect of Soviet life ...

For that to happen, science has to 'go nearer' to the masses. The adjectives high/low, broad/narrow, near/far, unilateral/multilateral have no real sense, but serve only to indicate a positive or negative connotation. They are used in an almost ritual fashion: 'near' designates the degree of closeness to the masses, 'broad' and 'high' refer to the speed and development of socialist production. In his novel, *1984* Orwell pointed to this feature of Newspeak in his witty way: 'Year by year and minute by minute, everybody and everything was whizzing rapidly upwards.' 'Broad', 'low' and 'high' can also describe moral or intellectual qualities.

In most cases, one term is opposed to the other. However, when Newspeak is used as an engine of war, – that is to say, during factional struggles inside the Party or in a purge – a positive term may be balanced against two negative ones, like an unattainable virtue caught between two indefinable but deadly vices. Thus patriotism can be achieved provided one avoids the pitfalls of chauvinism and cosmopolitanism. Today a true supporter of *perestroika* should avoid 'leftist phraseology' (*à la* Yeltsin) and 'negativism' (i.e. 'rejection of socialism'). In literature one should aim at realism by making strenuous efforts not to come to grief through naturalism or, even worse, formalism. The Party's function is to identify all the deviations from the correct line and to give them labels.

Every word in Newspeak is subjected to this manichean handling. Ideology throws all the words of ordinary language into a magnetic field where some are attracted to the positive pole and others to the negative.[18] Insidiously, value replaces meaning. Some of the peculiarities of syntax described earlier can be explained by this total polarisation of the language. For example, verbs are replaced by nouns because verbs are less easy to use in support of value-judgments. Every device is used to recruit the maximum number of words; and there is no doubt that it is this all-pervading polarisation which perverts the Newspeak vocabulary the most radically.[18]

Manicheism counts for a great deal in the specifically communist syntax and is the root, simultaneously, of its polemic vocabulary and aggressive use of words. However, the vocabulary of Newspeak is not restricted to the terminology of war. Other metaphors than military ones bring words in their wake:

The 'organic' metaphor

The most 'pregnant' metaphor is that of the organism, which underlies very many mannerisms of communist language and thought. It is of tremendous use to ideology, hence its widespread appearance in communist Newspeak as well as in the language of the Third Reich. '*Organichnyi*', like '*organisch*' has a strong positive connotation and is set against '*mekchanichny/mechanisch*'. Ideology needs the support of this metaphor to sanction its main contention. It is easy to see why: the idea of a living organism impresses on the mind the idea of determinism and above all of a natural force that is irresistible because unchangeable. It imposes on the human imagination a basic premise of ideology: the primacy of nature; not as it really is, but as something either good or bad and incapable of changing its spots no matter whatever may seem to happen. Then, surreptitiously, the image is moved from the biological world to the world of morality where it implants Manicheism. From evil, only evil can come; while a positive principle gives rise only to good. Thus, whatever happens, capitalism can only give birth to corruption; while socialism always results in good, however socialism is achieved. Historical development is like genetic programming. It proceeds as inevitably as an innate process. The fruits are already in the seeds, and the human will, good or bad, can do nothing to change them. And this is as true for societies as it is for individuals and principles: 'The ideas which were upheld by progressive thinkers in the 18th century contained, from the outset, the seed of conservatism. This produced, in the course of its later development, results diametrically opposed to the objectives which these great thinkers had sought sincerely to achieve.'

The organic metaphor informs a certain number of key ideas in Newspeak. The ideas of 'ripe' socialism and of the 'rotten' bourgeoisie; the concept of 'assimilation'; the Bolshevik idea of 'the nucleus' ('a solid nucleus of communists'). The organic metaphor engenders an unmistakable way of considering time, conceived first as 'development'; and above all the development that leads to 'the final stage'. Time is revealed as the continuum in which programmes are regularly fulfilled. History unfolds in accordance with the same inherent necessity as does a biological entity. Some Soviet texts go as far as to refer to 'naturalo-historic development'. There are no sudden transitions: 'What is new rises up from the depths of the old society'. The same continuity is to be found in philosophy: 'The teaching of Marx appeared as the direct continuation and development of the teachings of the world's greatest philosophers.'

History, then, is marked out by 'milestones' for those who know where to look for them. Newspeak is always at pains to point to these 'seeds', these 'young shoots', these 'germs' buried in the past – the 'compost from which revolution has sprung.' Proletarian eclecticism will select the positive elements from the past because: '*the absorption of every viable* tradition is a condition of progress itself.' That is why 'the internationalism of the working-class is saturated with all the best elements of the humanism of the Enlightenment.'

On the other hand, some superior minds were able to foresee the future long ago. Engels uttered 'words of prophecy'; 'Lenin's predictions have been fulfilled.' Even before that some bourgeois philosophers were able to come near the truth, although their class prejudices always limited their intuition and stopped them short.

> Following Feuerbach, Herzen *went further than Hegel* towards materialism ... he touched lightly on dialectical materialism but did not reach historical materialism.

Social life, like intellectual life, is part of this teleological movement, which figures in Newspeak in the form of countless phrases like 'already – but not yet':

> Among the spiritual fathers of the French bourgeois revolution the problem of patriotism was already very much bound up with that of democracy ... but one must never forget that patriotism is an ambiguous phenomenon in a class-based society. In the age when nations were being formed the patriotism of the popular classes, especially the proletariat, *was not yet* distinct from the patriotism of the bourgeoisie.

By means of this typical balancing of 'already' and 'not yet', the past is merged with the ideological vision. Judgments on contemporary issues are similarly merged, which demonstrates even more clearly the emphasis put on continuity:

> We *have never wavered* ... in our insistence on putting this question of democracy.[19]

> The political education of the workers *has always been* one of the basic tasks of the Communist party. At the present time, when the Soviet people are building a Communist society, that task has particular importance. The development among the workers of a vision of a Marxist-Leninist world *remains and will remain*[20] the central task of the ideological work of the party organisations.

The metaphor of the organism does not only support the idea of societies being bound by nature; for it not only encourages the belief in continuity – it also justifies social planning. Just as a biological entity follows its predetermined programme, so the social organism develops according to plans. In this lies the superiority of socialism. By planning the economy man assumes the role previously played by the physical world with its interplay of brutal laws. In a way, man steals a march on necessity by himself devising scientific plans for society's development.

The biological analogy invites a further distinction within each process: between 'steps', 'stages' and 'levels', which are strictly hierarchical of course; the most recent stage being also the most advanced one. The expressions 'at that time', 'at that moment', 'in the age of' refer to bygone and imperfect periods which progressive humanity has overtaken by a 'new step in its forward march' on the way towards 'a higher level'.

Mature socialism exhibits 'progressive development', in which 'giant steps' are no longer acceptable, but in which important advances can of course still take place. These stages are connected by 'transitional passages'. These are high points of dialectic. Each stage has its own types and achievements: how a society moves to the next stage is determined by the evolution of conditions. At any given moment assessments have to be made recalling the difficulties overcome, in order to sketch the way forward. The merits of each of the elements are then celebrated.

In this context two other key concepts of Newspeak become clearer: those of 'life' and 'creation'. 'Life' stands for the dynamism which implements the programmes, makes the laws of history come true and confirms the doctrine. 'Creation' refers to human activity seen from the same angle, i.e. activity which is in harmony with the trend of history and which helps to re-affirm the ideology.

'*Life* has refuted the predictions of the "predators".' '*Praxis* has confirmed the living strength of the Leninist position.' 'Socialism stems from *the creativity* of the masses.' 'As before, *life* strives forward.' The 'life-force' necessarily brings progress. And the classic writings of Marxism-Leninism are 'living sources'.

Now one can understand the expression 'creative analysis' which otherwise might well leave the uninitiated puzzled. All analysis is creative which introduces ideology into areas which previously it could hardly reach; or which can accommodate hostile facts so that they become ideologically acceptable. So Barbusse: 'In this way, perception becomes *creation*.'[21] So also the Bolshevik leader Kalanin:

> To be a Marxist is to be a *creator* ... without commitment of the soul, without *creation*, without a *living* and permanent involvement in everything that happens, Marxism would be only pseudo-marxism.[22]

We may note here that the concepts of 'life' and 'creation' have the same place in the language of the Third Reich.[23]

The immanent determination which the organic image sustains cannot always find expression in metaphor. There has to be a sociological concept too so as to express the loyalty of the social actors to their basic nature; in other words the ideology has to be 'ground' local determinism in a way consistent with global progress. Each protagonist must be sure to play his role correctly in the drama of history. It is the concept of 'basic' interests that fulfils this necessary function. It rivets classes and individuals to their nature, good or evil, pins them down in their essence and translates into the social field the sort of pertinacity which nature shows in organisms.

However only society itself and only social classes are

credited with specific nature which is innate and necessary:

The class war is the outcome of *innate and objective* laws.

What is *innate* in the bourgeoisie is foreign to the *social nature* of the working class.

As for the individual, he is shaped by external forces, which are purely mechanical. His upbringing determines his nature. Only in the second instance do his 'interests' play their part in fixing his position. We shall consider the place of the human will in Newspeak elsewhere.

The organic metaphor brings another valuable asset to Newspeak: it inspires the dialectic of 'the whole' and 'the part' – an invaluable and most serviceable addition to its armoury.

The ideology of the proletariat ... becomes all the more *organic* as it gives more and more consideration to *the general* and *the particular* to the 'part' and to the 'whole'.

The 'part' is obviously subordinate to the 'whole'. Without the whole, it is meaningless; detached from the whole, it dies. In Russian, the adjective *otdel'ny* (separate, isolated) embodies these assumptions: it means 'isolated from the whole', therefore 'of little importance'. It banishes to a secondary zone those negative aspects of socialism which Newspeak has to mention for one reason or another. So dissidents are referred to as 'isolated elements' and widespread poverty is called 'local shortages'. The Party alone has the privilege of the 'global approach'. It is the Party which watches over 'multilateral', 'homogeneous' Soviet society. Exploiting the organic analogy the Newspeak gives regular precedence to the one over the many. Thus at every level of his existence, New Soviet Man participates in the organic One: he lives in a classless society at peace with his conscience, quite unlike the bourgeois who is always at odds with himself.[24]

Organicity and the will: incarnation

Under its smooth surface, Newspeak hides a tension that is summed up in two words: 'development' and 'construction'. In spite of the march of history and the 'organically inevitable' man must intervene. But a world so deeply dedicated to 'highly-motivated processes' can hardly find room for man's efforts; so some of Newspeak's expressions betray the contradiction between the teleology of revolution and on the other the development that is based on will: 'In the friendly country of Poland the enemies of socialism *strive to divert development along* counter-revolutionary *lines*.'[25]

The task is to unite *in an organic whole* the achievements of science and the benefits of the socialist economic system.

True realism must have the power to direct *the progress of material things*.[26]

Material errors tend to rectify themselves, but the human spirit *must hasten his organic rectification*.[27]

Marxism shows up the depths and the *causal chains* of the logical contradictions of today's society and provides correct rules for analysing them ... Socialism is ... the doctrine which prints *out in advance the logical* needs of all and which each man *must work loyally to help bring about*.[29]

We have power in the measure that we understand and achieve the irresistible triumph of Marxism.[29]

Newspeak makes innumerable references to the unavoidable on the one hand, while on the other it piles up imperatives and exhortations:

Nations *must* exert themselves to achieve a common programme for the creation of the conditions which preserve peace

The need for these appeals for action becomes clear when one considers the social mode of 'natural evolution' in the ideological 'universe of wood'. The progress of history is described through the following 'concepts': 'flourishing', 'acceleration', 'consolidation', 'multiplication', 'development', 'reinforcement', 'deepening', 'increasing', 'taking off', 'enriching', 'expansion', 'unbridled growth', 'worsening', 'setting free', 'overtaking', 'spreading' – the list could be extended. In the context of these descriptions, human action, both individual and collective, can be seen in two ways – either as a continuing process already begun, or as the endeavour to effect a change in some development or other, especially by speeding it up or slowing it down.

Here are some of the verbs used to describe the possible ways in which man can participate in the vast progress of history: 'to foster, to play a part, to orientate, to facilitate, to create the conditions for, to put on the brakes, to perfect, to accelerate, to slow down, to stimulate, to rely on, to develop, to reinforce, to defend ...' And here are some typical expressions which define 'praxis':

In the future the Communist Party of the Soviet Union will continue its policy of *developing* cooperation with liberated countries.

To deepen its bonds (sic) with the mass of people.

To direct the energy of the masses along the lines of revolutionary struggle.

The Communist Party ... is *going ever deeper.*

To create the conditions essential to put an end to recession. (Of economic backwardness)

The Communists *have begun and will pursue an enormous activity* in the name of ...

So historical necessity is transformed surreptitiously into a moral imperative.[30] By simply acting in accord with history, an individual puts himself in the camp of the victors; while working with them towards the Good, he can speed up or anticipate progress. In that case, organic imagery no longer fits, and in order to gloss over the illegitimate modulation by which necessity becomes virtue, ideology has recourse to a venerable concept of such authority that its fundamentally non-materialist nature passes unnoticed. This is the idea of 'incarnation' – a pivotal gadget in the 'wooden' speechifying and a key element in the ideology itself.

It is this concept which forces on the mind the notorious 'law of unequal development' and serves to justify the existence of the Party. For, so the doctrine runs, society does not enjoy the regular organic growth of plant life: some of the elements it contains retard it. At the human level potentiality can, locally, be turned into actuality by means of successive purifications or purges. The word 'incarnation' signifies both the process by which the laws of history become actual and the progressive forces or 'avant garde' which speed up or anticipate the process. In this way the Party is legitimised, because it has already transcended potentiality and become actual, while its programmes have the power to draw the rest of society towards what has to be its destiny. Thus the concept of incarnation nullifies the contradiction between organic development and the exercise of the will. Small wonder that one finds it everywhere:-

The Communists are *flesh of the flesh*, *blood of the blood* of the working class.

The proletariat is the *personification* of the productivity of modern society.

Lenin is the ideal *incarnation* of the revolutionary.

The people's economic structure must *embody* the ideals of the new society, *put flesh* on the integration of science and production.

These ideas were broadly *incarnated* in life.

Materialism, however dialectical, has no terminology for expressing the emotionalism of emerging socialism or the revolutionary heroism of the avant-garde progressive. Here Newspeak is obliged to dip into the 'idealist' lexicon, and this limits the field of the organic metaphor.

The reflection and the form

The organic image has been pressed into service because it seems to provide the ideal, intelligible model of an all-embracing determinism. But the area the image covers is limited; not only because it is hard to integrate human action into a spontaneous evolving world bent on progress – but because the metaphor has an even more serious drawback. It presumes a principle of 'coherence' which is completely alien to ideology, which cannot even conceive of, much less concede, the morphological determinism of the living creature. Ideology stubbornly ignores the part played by forms in human individuation.

The world of forms is out of the ideology's reach for two reasons: first it is compartmentalized and thus totally resistant to any intellectual model of universal application. Second, the typical ideological approach, namely the movement away from appearance to an underlying, fore-known and unchanging essence – gives no grip on a universe of varied, solid external forms which exist and speak for themselves. It is through forms that existence shows its durability: and their presence in the world of the senses exposes the inanity of that fuzzy shadow world which ideology constructs beneath. The notion of 'formal' must therefore be destroyed. And it is here that 'incarnation' is so convenient. Incarnation evades the problem of change and form implicit in the organic metaphor by substituting the ideal for the form itself.

However, this internal coherence, the integrity of the ideological universe, relies on another concept, that of 'reflection'. This concept is essential to the proper function-ing of communist language because it alone makes it possible to graft the unreal hidden world onto 'particular' real phenomena that are chosen to receive it. 'Incarnation' serves as a launching-pad for the ideological hermeneutics. To reduce form to reflection, to discover under the treacherous multiplicity of forms, their true, unambiguous content is often the motivation of communist speech. Forms increasingly call to mind the vast extent of the world's hypocrisy, namely the masks it endlessly assumes to avoid the truth. It is forms, the doctrine teaches, which slow down progress, put the brakes on the march of history, confuse the consciousness of the masses and conceal the machina-tions of the class enemy: in short, forms hide Truth behind deceitful images which have to be cleared away. Phe-nomena have no real existence of their own; they only 'reflect'.

Consciousness, the ideology insists, is a reflection of the productive forces and of class relationships. The political structure reflects the interests of the ruling class. Art is a reflection of the revolutionary aspirations of the masses. The concept of reflection is primarily a way of expressing the ideology's basic malevolence. For it exposes the degenerate origins of phenomena. In Newspeak 'reflection' nourishes a whole catalogue of words and phrases which can either justify (if it is laws of history that support the reflection) or condemn (if the reflection is seen to serve the interests of the bourgeoisie). Here are some of these words and phrases which evoke the massive cohesion of a world held together by the doctrine of reflections: 'To reflect', ' to answer to'[31], 'to correspond to', 'to show through', 'to reveal itself in ' , 'to bear the marks of', 'to express the interests', 'to reflect the true situation'. Thus:

'All these characteristics *appear clearly* in ...'

'To *correspond with* the Marxist-Leninist view of historic processes.'

'The strategy of Marxist-Leninist parties best *fits* the needs of the developing world.'

'The influence of the international working class and the worldwide socialist system *shows itself* there also.'

'Centralised political control appears as *the reflection* of the natural economic unit.'

'This patriotism is *an indication of* the backward state of class-struggle.'

The concept of reflection escapes the manichean dichotomy because it is functional. It sustains the ideological approach and allows the return to principles, which is a fundamental part of the ideological method. The concept turns phenomena into representations and brings all the variety of the existing world within one unchanging theory. In the ideology reflection is not an analogy – that would leave it at the superficial and contemptible level of form – but a weapon which it uses to expand and conquer. Newspeak replaces real things with transparent ghosts through which the same unchanging principles remain easily visible. The concept of reflection greatly helps to sustain an illusion which fortifies ideology – the illusion that, thanks to ideology, everything in the world can be understood and all phenomena can be interpreted.

This however is not the only advantage 'reflection' confers. By promoting reflection to the status of a high principle, one has the intoxicating illusion of discovery, of having understood something new. And it is true that ideology imposes itself the more easily on the mind if it can convey an illusion of understanding, a promise of discovering the truth, the feeling of a knowledge which is gradually being unravelled. The denunciation of appearances by means of the reflection theory creates just such a delusion of discovery; and this justifies the claims of the ideologue.

From this viewpoint mental activity can take two forms: either it is a passive reflection or it actively detects reflections. Knowledge then becomes a matter of grasping the essence, good or bad, of phenomena which are themselves reduced to reflections. Thus the world of the ideologue is hidden behind numberless masks which it is vital to remove. From this a whole glossary of concealment and unmasking is derived: 'to pass itself off as', 'by pretending to care about', 'a false revolutionary', 'the hidden aspect', 'the action of unmasking', 'under the flag of'. And on every page you meet expressions like those:

'Reactionaries often *hide* the vilest sort of chauvinism *under* the guise of patriotism.'

'Here *is hidden* the economic basis of internationalism.'

'Radek said that whatever *veil* opportunism used to *conceal its* miserable body, he would see through it.'[32]

This idea of 'revealing', of gaining access to the reality behind the scenes, characterizes much of the vocabulary used to describe intellectual operations. Expressions like, 'uncover the deep nature (essence, substance)', 'penetrate to the depths of events' are in common use. In the ideology and its Newspeak, to think is to dismiss phenomena in order to concentrate on principles: for the ideologue, things, on the whole, are like words, a multiplicity of arbitrary signs that reveal a content that is definable by those who have a monopoly of understanding. In a world of appearances, ideas are not tied to external, stable being and form, but to the constant essence beneath. They serve as stepping-stones on the way to a hidden reality.

Studies devoted to ideological languages[33] always lay the main accent on vocabulary, especially on two of its characteristics: the polarisation of words and the lexical impoverishment. Many writers have noted that in ideological languages certain words acquire a value which is the opposite of that which they have in the everyday language of real life. For example, in the *lingua sovietica*, as in the language of the Third Reich, the word 'hate' has acquired a positive connotation: in both languages one can speak of 'holy hatred' or 'heroic hatred' and in the Nazi jargon '*fanatisch*' is considered a form of virtue. Among Bolsheviks 'blind faith' is a necessary virtue too. All these observations are very true but they do not account fully for the changes inflicted on natural vocabulary by the *langue de bois*. Inversion and simple suppression do occur but they do not determine the mechanism of Newspeak. The words of Newspeak, despite Orwell's view of it, do not always mean the opposite to what they mean in ordinary language. It would be more accurate to describe them as 'diverting' meaning from its true course. Take for example, the Newspeak word 'consciousness'. This word has no exact equivalent in natural language; for it means the extent to which one is permeated with ideology, i.e. is a 'politically conscious comrade' and hence denotes, by implication, more the *absence* than the presence of conscious in the normal sense. On the other hand, if Newspeak has suppressed very many words, very many words have been invented too, especially abbreviations and acronyms, without anyone's troubling at all about their barbarous effect. Those inventions include expressions like 'kolkhoz', 'liquidation of "cowlessness"', and 'the tendency towards problemlessness' (a characteristic of 'bureaucracy'). All these neologisms illustrate, in a sense, the lexical creativity of Newspeak.[34]

One needs, therefore, to dwell less on the impoverishment of the natural vocabulary than on the extreme poverty of the 'wooden' world of concepts. There a small number of vague but 'pregnant' images suffice to suck a whole glossary of words into the ideological orbit and to cast them down into nothingness. Ideology accepts a compromise with words: it lets them go on existing, having first emptied them of their meanings and injected them with a new content. Rather than abolish a concept, ideology ruins it, and thus achieves an even larger take over of ordinary language. Ideology reigns over a vocabulary which it has completely subverted and manipulated at will. Here one can really speak of the arbitrariness of the verbal sign.

STYLE

There is something almost ridiculous about applying the
term 'style' to the *langue de bois*. If one accepts the
common definition of style as the personal stamp which
each individual puts on language, one sees at once that
Communist speech is a 'non-style'. No text written in
Newspeak reveals the personality of its author, with the
possible exception of certain works of Stalin and Lenin. An
army of editors works on each text, polishing away until
Newspeak's verbal protocol is totally observed. Compared
with this thorough terminological inspection old-fashioned
censorship seems pretty home-spun: 'In the end we shall
make thought crime literally impossible because there will
be no words in which to express it,' declares Symes, the
inspired manufacturer of Newspeak in 1984. A truly
collective technique of writing is available in the Soviet
Union, which can be applied to any subject at all.

Rhetoric, Aristotle and Newspeak

Langue de bois claims to be pre-eminently a political
language. So let us try to apply to it the rules of classical
rhetoric, by means of which the orator seeks to win over his
listeners. In his *Rhetoric*, Aristotle enumerates the essential

ingredients of good style. To what extent does Newspeak
conform to them? Here are sentences taken at random from
a text devoted to the activities of Party organisations:

> In this matter the essential landmark for us is to be found in
> the resolutions of the recent report of the Central Commit-
> tee of the Communist Party of the Soviet Union: 'The
> eventual completion of control and of verification of the
> carrying out of work in the light of the decisions of the 26th
> Congress of the Communist Party of the Soviet Union.' It is
> a very important document regarding activities of Party
> organisations. In the light of its demands we must adopt a
> different approach, one more severe and more rigorous, to
> many aspects of Party activity.

Clarity

According to Aristotle the principal characteristic of good
style is clarity, because 'if the language does not clearly
reveal the subject, it will not fulfil its role'.[35] For a Western
reader the extract quoted above does not seem to say very
much: the Soviet reader will perhaps find more substance in
it, but only after working to interpret it in a way that has
nothing to do with the semantic processes of the language
itself. He makes a sort of interpretation of it.

In itself Newspeak is vague, full of abstractions and
tautology: it avoids precision. If there is any clarity to be
found in 'wooden' texts, it certainly owes nothing to stylistic
merit. A great deal of practice is required before one can
extract any sense. In Newspeak, a language frozen into
immutable patterns, each noun has its obligatory adjective,
each verb its conventional complement; and if there is any
irregularity in the ritualized forms it has an ulterior
meaning. The choice of subject-matter may actually be
more significant than what is said about it. A text whose
real meaning lies in its divagations from an implicit formula

is very far from being clear in the sense intended by Aristotle.

Aptness

'Aptness' is the second characteristic of good style. A speaker must adapt his words to his subject and take account of his audience and the effect he is making. 'Style must be neither too mundane nor too high-flown: it must be appropriate.' It was on this idea of aptness that Cicero based his theory of the three styles appropriate to the objectives of an orator: to prove, to please or to move. Here are some quotations, from different writers and refering to different subjects.

Definite progress has been made towards defining the nature of cybernetics since the meeting on 14th May 1980 of the philosophy section of the Science Council, which was devoted to the complex problem of 'Cybernetics'. Academician B.N. Petrov, president of the Science Council, emphasized the necessity, felt at the present time, of achieving a definition of cybernetics which would be more precise and therefore of greater consequence and in a sense more restrictive.[36]

The widespread interest which is being shown everywhere favours the rapid development of the science of demography which is more and more decisively overcoming the narrow confines of its applications and seeking to provide a more detailed and profound vision of the nature of the processes with which it is concerned. This tendency is linked to a growing desire to achieve a more exact theoretical understanding of the *differentia specifica* of the particular area of social reality in which those processes take place.'[37]

In the decisions of the 26th Congress of the Communist Party of the Soviet Union all aspects of the growing link between economics and sociology under conditions of developed socialism have been brought into the light. On the one hand, the basis for a solution of social problems lies within the scope of economics. The principal objective of the Party's economic strategy – a fuller use of the intensive factors of economic development – is being pursued resolutely for the sake of increasing the well-being of the people. On the other hand, progress towards a truly intensive system of economic development requires a considerable increase in the part played by those social factors which enhance the improvement of the efficacy and of the quality of commercial output.'[38]

The aesthetic categories of the good and the sublime, tragedy and comedy, etc., were shaped historically as man gradually absorbed into his practical and artistic activities the corresponding external qualities he found in natural and social reality. This process cannot be regarded as being finished in any historical period.[39]

Those quotations show that the style is absolutely identical whoever the author is and whatever his subject. The subject is simply flattened under the steamroller of the 'wooden style'; anybody who has mastered Newspeak can write it for pages, or make a speech on any topic, without knowing the first thing about the subject. There is no distinction between written and spoken styles. 'Wooden' speech is adapted as little to its audience as 'wooden' writing is to its theme. In any case, there is no need; for the appropriate response is often indicated in advance. When the Soviet citizen reads: 'The Soviet people learned of the decisions of the ... Congress with great enthusiasm', he knows exactly what is expected of him.

Nevertheless, there *is* a kind of aptness within Newspeak, although it is very remote from the 'aptness' of Classical eloquence. It is the aptness with which words are arranged in conformity with a prescribed ritual which everyone understands. This is a purely internal conformity which refers only to the bare mechanisms of the language itself.

Invention

A good style means not only clarity and aptness: it must also surprise by bringing up unexpected elements which will hold the listener's attention. 'And so one must give to language a novel quality, because the exotic is always appreciated ... style should have a remote quality; it should conceal its technique while always remaining clear.' – so Aristotle tells us. Here once again, Newspeak exhibits ambivalence. A rigid verbal protocol governs the *langue de bois* which would seem to rule out any novelty immediately. The obligatory fictions of ideology do indeed prohibit the individual imagination. But even Newspeak cannot avoid invention altogether; for it is a kind of language that has always to hide its true nature. Invention is therefore the ensemble of methods by which it hides itself.

Aristotle left us also a list of those qualities which made up a bad style. It is interesting to confront Newspeak with Aristotle's criteria:-

The misuse of compound words: this occurs frequently in Newspeak, as we have seen.

The misuse of neologisms: this also happens in Newspeak, as does the third fault mentioned by Aristotle:

'*Periphrasis*, when used at excessive length, or inappropriately, or too often.' Thus, Lenin is always 'the great leader of the proletariat of the world'; the Party, 'the progressive vanguard of the working class'.

Bogus metaphors, that is, those which are not based on a genuine analogy and are consequently inappropriate. In this connexion one has only to remember the bizarre imagery of Communist speech, from 'the iron battalions of the pro-letariat' to 'the bestial grimace of capitalism', not to mention cacophonies such as 'The fascist octopus has sung his swan song',[40] 'having thrown away the fig-leaf of neo-colonialism, imperialism at last reveals its true face'.[41]

Or, to use examples from Barbusse, who again wins first prize:

The hopes of the capitalists danced furiously on the still open wounds of the murdered people. (Barbusse, 1935, p. 160)

Planning and electrification expand their theoretical and practical tide, in waves. (Ibid, p. 176)

Lenin and Marx are two great concentric personalities, who evolved in the framework set up by the elder of them. (Ibid, p. 43)

To unfreeze our theory with slogans capable of setting the workers on fire. (Ibid, p. 49)

Theory provides the path from start to finish. If it is correct, it has a line to the future. (Ibid, p. 172)

Electrification was the solid root which brought the whole vision of industry down to earth. (Ibid, p. 160)

Aristotle's final principle concerns diction: 'What one has written should be easy to read and to say.' The well-known difficulties which Brezhnev experienced with some of his sentences were not only due to ill-health. Some 'wooden' phrases are simply unpronouncable. They are a source of many jokes among Russians. Thus, judged by standards of classical eloquence, Newspeak is characterized by a truly bad style. What this means, however, is that those standards are simply not appropriate to the language of ideology, which entirely differs from classical rhetoric in its aims. For ideology does *not* seek to please. It does *not* feel any need to prove anything, because everything has been settled once and for all, by the founding fathers of Marxism-Leninism. All that remains is to do some fine-tuning. Nor does ideology make any effort to move the emotions, for what are the vain affectations of language beside the splendour of the Truth it conveys? Through the perfect organization of its verbal ritual *langue de bois* deliberately represents the subjection of the world to history's inescapable progress. It is a mimicry of the very laws that it states, for ideological truth has to be conveyed immediately to the understanding. Newspeak aims at what Alexander Zinoviev calls the 'scientoid' style. From the language of science it borrows a style full of nouns, which avoids verbs, is easy to write, is vague about time, facilitates impersonality, is remote from the spoken word and kept in quarantine against the contagion of real language and real life. Hence the stylistic monstrosity of Newspeak, the length and obscurity of its sentences, the dull syntax and the deadly overall monotony.

Hyperbole and euphemism

There is, however, one area where Newspeak says an emphatic good-bye to the scientific style and betrays its intimate connexion with ideology. For each of its state-ments implies a value-judgment. Each proposition is biased. Time and again aggressivity pervades the language, which it oscillates mostly between invective and eulogy, oblivious of the threat to its ostensible objectivity.

When Newspeak sheds the 'scientoid' style, it swings also between the vulgar and the lofty. The scale of the communist insult system is well-known: lackeys of imperialism mingle with fascist cannibals in low cosmopolitan dives; or break into anti-soviet orgies urged on by the worshippers of the golden calf. Confronting them, the proletariat carries on its heroic struggle under the wise guidance of the great Communist Party, inspired by the sublime thoughts of that genial guide of the working class, the immortal V.I. Lenin. Orwell commented on the artificiality and lack of spontaneity of this abuse: he believed that the insults were translated from the Russian, and that in Russian[42] this rang true. In fact, however, these terms of abuse are never used in everyday Russian in which they give the same impression of turgid incongruity as they do in English. When it attempts poetic fervour Newspeak does make use of figures of speech, but they are so worn that their effect is blunted. The metaphors are 'dying'[43] because worn out: the same metonymies invariably indicate the enemy or glory of the forces of progress. 'Wall Street' or 'the Pentagon' serve as labels for the reactionary camp, while the banner of Socialism heralds the presence of the Good. The same lifelessness overcomes adjectives, which become victims of what Klemperer called 'the curse of the superlative'.[44] An expression as ridiculous as 'the most first' which occurred in *Pravda* shows how far the emotional charge can prevail over the sense, and how it has to be verbalised whatever the cost.

As well as hyperbole, Newspeak regularly uses euphemism – the latter nearly always follows on from the former. The structure of communist texts is in itself as much a cliché as the figures of speech it carries. The text can be compared to a pendulum, whose swing is enough to betray the 'wooden' style. One starts with a pretentious glorification of various successes achieved in the given area. Words or expressions with inoffensive connotations, such as 'however', 'unfortunately', 'everyone knows', 'there is no need to refuse to see that there still exist ... ' follow the opening purple passage. The tone changes and one is into the euphemisms: it becomes a matter of 'difficulties', of a 'complex situation', of 'negative phenomena'. Finally pendular equilibrium is restored as measures are announced which will do away with these occasional drawbacks and defects:

> The process of bringing mature socialism to perfection becomes more and more widespread ... *However*, this process has not been without some difficulties, arising from the lack of agricultural development in the country and the worsening international situation. Nevertheless its main objectives have, nonetheless, been successfully attained.

Indeed Newspeak can only function by passing its verbal current between the opposite poles of hyperbole and euphemism. The only stable balance it can achieve lies in tautology. For as soon as the artificial tension of hyperbole is released, as soon as the aim to restore the status quo is fulfilled, Newspeak gets bogged down in repetition. This proclivity is so much a part of its nature that a great many tautologies escape the watchful eye of the editor.

These tautologies are interesting because often they reveal the natural tendencies of Newspeak, and for that reason go unnoticed. So Stalin spoke of 'semantic meaning', Bakhtin of 'summing-up résumés': elsewhere it is a quotation of 'the origins of the beginning' or the 'aims of objectives'. And since Gorbachev came to power much stress is laid on the 'potential possibilities' of socialism.

The elusiveness of the ideological style, which now imitates scientific discourse, now tends towards polemics; the banality and confusion of its metaphors, the lack in it of a sense of proportion and, even more, the tendency to tautology – all these features point to one conclusion: in Newspeak thought has deserted speech.

Whence the difficulty of defining the 'wooden' style according to criteria borrowed from classical writers. In the ordinary course of events, language accompanies thought and shapes it. In its search for words, thought gains in clarity and distinctness. Style bears the imprint of thought upon its trajectory. The result is a compromise between thought's dynamism and the stability imposed by words. With Newspeak, however, there is no longer anything to think about: all the thinking has already been done once and for all. Language no longer has anyone or anything to accompany and can only trudge its solitary way on paths whose smallest windings are known by heart to everyone. No longer is language at the birth of an idea, nor does it help to formulate one: its function is to sound the echo of the original, definitive statements of the Founding Fathers. Newspeak travels for ever in the wake of offical scripture, reproducing itself automatically by means of tested formulae parroting a remote and bygone message. Without the discipline of new thought, language is bound to follow its meanest tendencies. It avoids the concrete, abuses words, misuses circumlocution, neglects the principle of economy, deforms syntax, and dresses itself up in a jumble of technical, administrative and archaic terms. This is why emotionalism swells so hugely within Newspeak. It is the stylistic index of that loss of value which affects words when they float about freely, unanchored in thought. When it is unconstrained by thought or reality, language suffers an infinite inflation. Then its imposture is revealed: through its pomposity, its grandiloquence, through the disproportion of its words and its bogus logical articulations. As soon as language ceases to be the cloak of thought, it clothes only a ghost and its frantic efforts at aggrandisement are simply attempts to hide its emptiness.

Communist Newspeak, is, then, a unique and vivid example of a language which has cut itself off from thought, but has not died of the split. It has not died because it is artificially kept alive by totalitarian political power or by the ideology that envelops it. But a language turned in on itself becomes, inevitably, a self parody. In a normal society it must either reform itself or die. From the start Soviet Newspeak has been stalked by parody. Only terror – mental at first then political – and the will to power have prevented the force of parody from wrecking the language's mechanism of perpetual movement. But we still have to see how the language protects itself and manages to survive.

Notes to Introduction and Chapter I

[1] Translator's note: There is no equivalent in English of the French *langue de bois*; on balance I prefer to use Orwell's term 'Newspeak', although this term does not express the dead, contrived quality of 'langue de bois', which might also be rendered as 'Deadspeak'.

[2] By 'ideology' I mean a form of gnostic thought which claims to provide a scientific basis for a doctrine of salvation. In the twentieth century Marxism-Leninism and Nazism are its most finished forms. For the definition of ideology, see A. Besançon, *The Intellectual Origins of Leninism*.

[3] This study deals with the standardised forms of communist language as a whole. The examples I have chosen are taken from the Soviet press and French communist publications, mostly for their routine character. The English reader can get an idea of Soviet language by looking at the English publications of the Novosti Press Agency, Moscow.

[4] H. Barbusse, *Staline*, Paris, 1935, p. 282.

[5] '*Humanité*', 26 February, 1968

[6] Paul Valéry, *Cahiers I*, Gallimard, 1973, p. 455.

[7] For further reading on this notion of 'enunciation' (*énunciation*), shifters (*embrayeurs*), and the analysis of pronouns, see E. Benveniste, *Problèmes de linguistique générale*, Paris, 1966, pp. 251 onwards.

[8] R. Jakobson, *Essais de linguistique générale*, Paris, 1963, vol. 1, p.178.

[9] H. Barbusse, *op.cit.* 1935, p.234.

[10] G. Marchais, preface to *Programme commun de gouvernement*, Paris, 1972, p.13.

[11] Ibid, p.21.

[12] Marchais, Ibida, pp. 37-38.

[13] An enquiry undertaken by Soviet writers has shown that journalists use about 1500 words, while *Dal'* contains 220,000. See V. Belov *"Yazyk moy, drug moy"* in: *Nash Sovremennik*, No. 7, 1983, pp. 181-187. (*Dal'* is a 19th century dictionary of Russian, equivalent to *Littré*.)

[14] This characteristic of Newspeak is stressed by all the studies which have been made of it. See especially A.M. Selishchev, *Yazyk revoliutsionnoi epochi*, Moscow, 1928, pp. 94-95.

[15] In this connection, see Cornelia Berning, *Vom "Abstammung-nachweis" zum "Zuchtwart". Vokabular des Nationalsozialismus*, Berlin, 1964.

[16] In this connection, see Theodor Pelster, *Die politische Rade im Western und Osten Deutschlands*, Düsseldorf, 1966.

[17] The first two examples are taken from L. Rzevsky, *Yazyk i totalitarizm*, Munich, 1951.

[18] Researchers interested in the study of Newspeak have nearly always been struck by this polarisation of concepts. On this interesting subject, see the report of a secret symposium on the subject of Newspeak held in Warsaw in 1978: *Jezyk Propagandy*, Warsaw 1978. See also other articles inspired by the symposium: Leszek Bednarczuk, *'Wadza nad mówa'*, in *Pismo 2*, April 1981, pp. 93-102; Andrzej Luczaj, *'Zniewolony jezy'*, in *Kultura 12*, 1980, pp. 100-106. Mr. Bronski, *'Totalitarny jezyk Kommunismu'* in *Kultura 12*, 1979, pp. 91-99. Mr. Heller, *'Jezyk sowiecki a jezyk rosyjski'* in *Kultura 12*, 1979, pp. 99-103. See also the excellent article by R. Gandig, *Die Deutsche Sprachspaltung'* in *Neue deutsche Hefte*, Vol. 55, February 1959, pp. 1008-1014.

[19] G. Marchais, *Humanité*, 17 March, 1984.

[20] This phrase became a *sine qua non* of all 'wooden language' statements made during Brezhnev's regime.

[21] H. Barbusse, 1935, p.59.

[22] M.I. Kalinin, *O Vospitanii Kommunisticheskoi soznatel' nosti*, Moscow, 1946, p.13.

[23] Cf especially *'schöpferisch'* (creative), *'schaffend'* (creating), *'lebensgesetzlich'* (in accordance with the laws of life).

[24] The Nazis had the same idea of harmony within the whole, using it, paradoxically, to *deny* the necessity of class war.

[25] An expression used by the linguist, N.J. Marr.

[26] H. Barbusse, 1935, p.94.

[27] Ibid, p.26.

[28] Ibid, p.25.

[29] Ibid, P.173.

[30] Kolakowski has made a penetrating analysis of this particular Marxist ambiguity, which claims to derive a teleology and a moral norm from a 'scientifically objective' account. See L. Kolakowski, *L'Esprit révolutionnaire*, Brussels, 1978.

[31] Translator's note: as in 'answers to the description'.

[32] H. Barbusse, 1935, p.201.

[33] In this connection see the excellent article by Otto B. Rogele *'Die Spaltung der Sprache'* in *Die politische Meinung*, *Heft*, 36, May 1959, R. Gaudig, 1959, and a work on the language of the Third Reich, which contains many interesting comments: V. Klemperer, *Die unbewaltigte Sprache*, Darmstadt, 1956.

[34] For Soviet neologisms, see L. Rzhevskiy, 1951, pp. 8, 9.

[35] Aristotle, *Rhetoric*, III, 2, 1404 b, on.

[36] N.T. Abramova, in *Voprosy Filosofii*, 1981, no.3, p.71.

[37] A.G. Visparevsky, Ibid, 1981, no.4, p.71.

[38] V.S. Rogvin, Ibid, 1981, no.6, p.3.

[39] V.P. Krutous, Ibid, 1981, no.6, p.125.

[40] Quoted in G. Orwell: 'Politics and the English Language' in *The Collected Essays, Journalism and Letters*, Penguin Books, Vol.4, p.164.

[41] This example was given to me by a translator of A P N (*Novosti Press Agency*).

[42] G. Orwell, 1970, vol. III, pp.132-135.

[43] G. Orwell, 1970, vol. IV, p.159.

[44] On the excess of superlatives in Soviet language, see A.M. Selishchev, 1928, pp.128-129.

II

HOW NEWSPEAK WORKS

... Language also comprises a technique by means of which one can ... deliver spoken fictions of all things ... which convey the impression that ... the speaker knows everything better than anyone else.

To appear and seem to be without actually being, to say things without actually saying the Truth – these are ways of proceeding which give rise to much embarrassment.

Plato, *Sophist*

Once again, Marxism teaches us: a word is a word, that is to say, nothing in itself.

H. Barbusse, *Stalin*

Newspeak conveys no new ideas and describes nothing whatever. However, the Communist Party and the totalitarian State cannot do without it because it serves to maintain ideology's fictions, to bring them up-to-date and to protect the ideology from the malevolent attack of real things. Newspeak identifies the 'weak links' in the real world and replaces them by its own hinges of wood. Likewise, it repairs the fissures made by reality in the protective netting of ideology. This netting must always be kept intact, otherwise it may be completely unravelled. Newspeak makes these running repairs possible and guarantees the permanent renewal without which ideology would lose its virulence and its whole grip on the world.

Even at the height of terror, when there is no danger from the opposition, *langue de bois* continues to grind out its refutations to people who are dumb with fear. Plato remarked about the disciples of Parmenides, who argued for the unchanging One, and those of Heraclitus, who argued for universal change: 'They have no need of external critics, for, as it is said, they carry their enemies and their opponents lodged in their hearts and they take the nagging internal voice, in the fashion of the eccentric Eurycles, wherever they go.'[1]

That comment fits the communists perfectly; for they must simultaneously refute everything that is and everything that might be. This explains their need for an inexhaustible flow of words, both defensive and aggressive, to serve at the same time as shield and as sword. Newspeak defends itself against things and attacks people. Once people are reduced to silence or, better still, to Newspeak, *langue de bois* has to face up to the counter-attack from reality. Here, as with all 'ideo products', Newspeak disposes of a very flexible tactic. According to circumstances it will range from an apparently unfavourable compromise with ordinary language – a compromise which can even look like defeat – to an arrogant and insolent affirmation of its own dialectical superiority.

The preceding chapter has been devoted to what we might call ceremonial Newspeak: the language of wood at rest; that is, a sort of ideal Newspeak. It must be emphasised, however, that Newspeak can take on other forms when circumstances demand it.

Any reader of *Pravda* or *l'Humanité* can see that his paper is not completely written in the language described in the first chapter. The editorial language represents only the culminating stage of Newspeak – the happy state when it can operate without any content at all. Nothing more would be needed if ideology was obliged only to cover reality up and dress it in a vaguely rebarbative mythology. But this is not all. Reality has to be assimilated, digested or at the very least minced up into unrecognisable forms.

We now turn, therefore, to the stages of the assimilation process. Here we discover a remarkable phenomenon: a language which is entirely devoted to the destruction of reality, but which at the same time (in typically Leninist fashion) also makes use of reality. This rare phenomenon deserves close scrutiny.

THE PRELIMINARY TREATMENT OF REALITY

The purpose of this first phase is essentially to shatter the coherence of the real world in order to replace it with Marxist-Leninist structures. To break up obstinate facts, several tactics can be used. They may be suppressed from the outset. This indeed is the method most often used. Facts and events are divided into categories; and those facts whose integration within the ideological framework would cause more damage than benefit to it are simply suppressed. Also suppressed or glossed over are those facts which demonstrate the (absurd) ideological neutrality of the real-life physical world. Thus the Soviet press more often than not omits to mention natural disasters and accidents, to the great astonishment of the West.[2] Such events, of course, are of no ideological use and may even be harmful in that they publicize the unpredictability of things. So they are simply not mentioned, which is the fate of most events unfavourable to the progressive camp. The suppressive technique has been widely used. Glasnost notwithstanding, matters considered by Soviet officials to be of vital interest are still consigned to virtual silence. Thus the press has been remarkably reticent about America; as it was, until the propaganda value of 'open-ness' was perceived, about Chernobyl. Besides, the technique of suppression makes it much easier to apply the second tactic, which is to transform certain events into illustrations. Some fact is selected and isolated from its context by means of the sifting and suppressing. It is then highlighted against the vacuum already created around it. The isolated fact can then be used to support the claims of ideology as an illustration *a posteriori* of axioms already thoroughly verified. For example the Soviet press will only select certain dramatic details of life in the West: old people freezing to death in a garret, fathers of families thrown out of work, queues outside Poilane (Paris's luxury baker) – details all suited to demonstrate once more the thesis of capitalism's decline.

The selection of 'typical' facts is not always arbitrary: thus when a Soviet citizen reads in his paper that the price of bread in France has gone up again, he prepares himself for a new bout of inflation in his own country and wonders anxiously which prices are going to increase. But there is never a clear and predictable relationship between a fact chosen by the Soviet Press and an element of reality. With practice one can guess at the *probable* motive; but it is always hard to decide whether a fact is chosen for its illustrative value or whether it is intended as a diversion. This is another common tactic of ideology.

The diversion is a sort of catharsis, as it were an emptying out of evil, at the end of which all the world's negative elements – such as infringements of human rights, economic disasters, and military adventures –are put back in their rightful place, namely the corrupt world of capitalism. A successful diversion makes it possible to drive out all the evils of life and ascribe them to the opposite camp. It provides answers to the most serious objections of that silent critic, reality. Thus Soviet citizens could read in the *Literary Gazette* of 28 April 1976 that in Italy, people of perfectly sound mind were being shut up in psychiatric hospitals for no other wrongdoing than criticizing the government, the judges and the police; or for displeasing their rich and influential parents. The unsavoury details given by the paper were overwhelming: not only were the unfortunate people interned by force, they were made to work for a pittance. Some months later (29 September 1976) the same journal denounced similar abuses in the United States, where ostensibly ill people were tortured without hesitation. On 11 March 1981, at a time when the Reagan administration was accusing the Soviet Union of international terrorist activities, the headline in the *Literary Gazette* read: 'Terrorism is the arm of imperialism'.

Following the events in Poland, however, the ideological situation became so serious that the authorities made a remarkable concession. The media were allowed to indulge in sensation for its own sake, as it was absolutely necessary to capture the attention of the masses. But this time no 'political' diversion could do the trick. Soviet citizens were therefore suddenly given the right to know about a bizarre and exciting incident at home, which was blown up to a most unusual degree. A family in Baku had raised a lion for many years, until one fine day the animal, in murderous fury, ate the son of the family and seriously injured the mother. Its capture was full of drama. This incident fuelled a vigorous debate, skilfully managed by the press, which, it seems, captivated the minds of the readers.[3]

This example shows how far Newspeak can renounce its principles when circumstances make it necessary. The events in Poland had jeopardised the very foundations of the ideological empire; hence extreme measures were needed to push them to the back of the citizens' minds. The ravenous lion was a spectacular example of a desperate method. There again, Newspeak derives an enormous advantage from its ceremoniality. Every break from the norm has an immense impact. After Solidarity's defeat, the ritual order duly returned and diversions once again became drearily ideological. As usual they consisted of boomerangs onto the opposite camp of accusations against the Soviet

Union itself of which Soviet newspaper-readers are some-times unaware. Thus the *Literary Gazette* of 22 December 1982 informed its readers that the United States was about to carry out experiments in bacteriological warfare in Pakistan, meaning not far from Afghanistan.

The undoubted efficacy of these three processes means that Newspeak has to resort less often than is supposed to the most obvious tactic: the lie. The lie after all presupposes a truth from which one departs: it is local and can easily be tracked down. It rests on a reality which it cannot destroy. The coarse ideological method of the lie was much respected in Stalin's day, when the most fantastic fabrica-tions were possible. But mature socialism rejects this showy and obvious method, partly, perhaps, because Western radio broadcasts now play such a large part in informing the Soviet people. Socialism has had to move on to more subtle falsifications in which a small amount of truth insinuates a mass of falsehood along with it. Newspeak simply encour-ages people to draw incorrect inferences: while it subtly distorts reasoning, opens up false perspectives and surrepti-tiously closes the many paths that do lead to truth.

Saint Augustine defines the lie in a way which fully applies to Newspeak: 'It is the intention, not the truth or falsity of the matter itself, that allows us to decide whether someone is lying or not ... One can be lying even when what one says is true ... To lie is to speak against one's own thought with the intention of deceiving ...'[4] Whenever Newspeak uses one of these methods, (illustration, diver-sion or lies) it tries to pass itself off as ordinary natural language. It will use anecdotes, flesh-and-blood heroes, picturesque descriptions, animated dialogue. When News-peak is most aggressive, it knows how to make such considerable formal concessions. Then Newspeak's only identifiable feature is its naked will to defend the ideology at any cost. It never lies more – by Saint Augustine's standards – than when it puts aside its conventional canons and disguises itself as a reporter of truth.

This tactic needs closer examination. For the communist ideology Poland and Afghanistan are two particularly indigestible morsels. From 1980 - 1983, events in those countries therefore occasioned some of Newspeak's most spectacular contortions. Most often the effect of truthfulness is created by introducing a narrator, who as a rule is a Soviet reporter wandering across foreign lands, rather like Gulliver, interested in everything and meeting horrors at every step. He describes his discoveries in a tone of false *bonhomie*, but the reader senses that his broadmindedness is constantly put to the test. Sometimes his resentment shows through, his patience gives way, he is outraged; he then explicitly challenges the 'capitalist gentlemen' who are invariably malicious and wicked. Most of the diversions are presented in this way. For illustrations, the Soviet media allow themselves from time to time, the luxury of quoting from the bourgeois Press.

One gets an idea of the infinite inventiveness of Newspeak when one reads its articles about Afghanistan during the first years of the war. The life of the Soviet troops is described in a quite pastoral manner. The Soviet press is full of touching little descriptions in which the brave Afghan peasant, his back bent under a thousand-year old oppression, fixes his radiant gaze on his brand-new tractor. The Soviet correspondent who portrays this idyllic scene does not pass up the chance of conversing with this representative of the peasant masses. The peasant makes clear that Soviet soldiers are very friendly and shakes hands with them to mark the occasion. Here is a sample of this kind of prose, taken from the *Literary Gazette* of 11 February, 1981:

... A dry field, hard and grey, covered with thorny pink bushes left after the cotton harvest. Beside him stands another, younger, peasant wearing brown baggy trousers ...

he is the owner of the land: the old man in the turban is his father ... The young man was given these two hectares during the land reform. Fifteen people have to live off its crop and father is regarded as a poor man, but he never goes hungry. If, God forbid, there are still robbers to steal part of his harvest, his family's livelihood will be gone. But now there is no risk, robbers do not venture into the region and the peasants know how to protect their harvest ... No, he is not a member of the cooperative, his father forbids it ... He himself would like to enter the cooperative, in order to rent a tractor and obtain some seed ... look at the tanned faces of these Afghan peasants who ... have endured monarchies, invasions, changes of religion and government, and reflect: what a sturdy breed, what a robust psychology, how well adapted for survival! ... But changes have come, the peasant mind is advancing ... I walk in the villages; I breathe the peaceful smoke of their fires; I watch them prepare the earth for water and seed. I know: somewhere there is the sound of gunfire, the killing continues. But all that will pass – these people look forward to working in peace.

Alexander Prohanov

Superficially, Newspeak appears on the scene incognito. There is, it seems, no turning away from the concrete, no noun phrases, no direct imperatives, no comparatives. The style is sharp and lively. And yet, 'wooden' characteristics are still there, almost all of them. Once more one finds the antithesis of past and future represented allegorically by the father and son, the father preventing his son from joining the cooperative: the unstoppable march of progress. One finds the futile attempts by enemies defined predictably as 'bandits' and 'robbers', duly marginalised by contrast with the hostile working people. In fact, this apparently realistic description is no more than a prescription of what must be, by virtue of the laws of history and for the good of humanity – Newspeak has simply resorted to socialist realism.

Poland is treated differently. This unfortunate country is the victim of machinations plotted outside its borders. So our fearless Soviet reporter takes himself to the heart of the enemy to investigate. He visits shady offices in London, New York or Munich where agents of every shape and size stir up trouble in Poland. Because he looks so honest, these agents accept him as a confidant and tell him the detail of the fiendish plots which will thrust Poland out of the socialist camp. The *Literary Gazette* of 7 January 1981 relates one of these courageous forays:

The proprietor of a company called 'Tazab', Tadeusz Zablocki, received me; because of a misunderstanding he took me for an Italian journalist and I didn't correct him.
– How is business, Mr Zablocki?
– There's so much work I just haven't a moment. Since the happenings in Poland began we are sending five times as many goods there. And now the press is interested! Yesterday I had an interview with *Newsweek*, this morning it was German television and now you ...
– I believe you have agreed, by telephone, to accept some packages from the United States?
– Yes, we now have important clients in the U.S.A., Canada and West Germany.
– Suppose someone brought you a crate of machine guns and asked you to despatch them there ...?
Zablocki flashed a patronising smile as if to say "you don't know the half of it, laddie".
– We are a hundred per cent anti-Communist, he said. But we have to be careful. The Polish Customs could suddenly decide to take a look in the crates ...
Eventually my interviewee could no longer keep his secret and blurted it out:
– And who, in your opinion, am I? A professional exporter? No! At one time ... he solemnly adjusted his bow tie ... I had the honour to be a Press Officer in our government in London after the Communists had got the upper hand in Poland ...
At which point Zablocki made a proud but clumsy movement with his hand, like an old crow who spreads his wings to reassure himself that he can still fly.

Vl. Simonov

In this example too Newspeak tries hard to imitate
ordinary language, using everyday phrases, and here and
there slipping into details taken from real-life. Yet the style
gives itself away, in the first place by the zeal with which it
tries to prove too much and to pile up improbable
insinuations, but most of all by the irresistible force which
pushes the writer into allegory. The wording of our extract
is typical: a comparison apparently inspired by physical
details turns itself without any warning into a symbol which
amounts to a threat. The spurious ornaments behind which
the language of wood has been concealing itself vanish in an
instant and it is shown that the *dramatis personae* are no
more than puppets expressing without conviction the forces
behind them.

All these processes have the same object: to take away
from phenomena their intrinsic intelligibility. The act of
omission allows the writer to spirit away the real connexions
between events and to conceal their causes. Diversion
enables false comparisons, illusory analogies and all sorts of
sleight of hand. Illustration twists the appearance of things
and destroys all sense of proportion. Newspeak is much
more than a clever tissue of lies. It takes great care to
arrange the scenery in which it places its inventions, then it
dresses them up in the cast-off rags of forbidden reality. All
Newspeak has an open mode – ceremonial Newspeak which
we described in the first chapter – and a hidden mode that
could be called 'the pseudo-natural language'[5] used in false
reporting as well as in false literature. The hidden mode
turns Newspeak into a true Leninist instrument, it allows
the user to adapt to any circumstances and above all to
mount attacks which are all the more effective for being
hidden.[6] For it is at the moment of reverting to ordinary
language, and of seeming to renounce the ceremonial
canons that Newspeak is most vigorous in its attack upon
reality.[7]

This raises a question, however: how does Newspeak furnish the empty world which emerges from such a screening; and how does it substantiate its own scheme of intelligibility?

HOW NEWSPEAK ASSIMILATES REALITY

The false differentiation of the content

Articles written in the pseudo-natural language by no means predominate in Soviet newspapers: here ceremonial Newspeak takes the lion's share. It is in this language that all the false events fed to the press are described. Soviet newspapers tend to be smaller than ours, but they have to fill up their columns all the same. The systematic practice of omitting and excluding everyday small events would seem to make the editor's task more difficult. But this is not so: the Soviet press has a knack of finding pretexts for what it writes. What then are the 'pegs' for its routine comment?

Each day brings its solemn occasions. Sometimes it will be a factory's exceeding the production targets fixed by the plan; which factory finds itself honoured by the Order of the Red Banner bestowed by Comrade So-and-So, who makes a speech emphasizing the need for harder work. This comrade is answered by a worker-delegate keen to tell him of all the precious experience which the collective has gained. At another time it is a visit from a Head of State, who emphasizes the urgency of friendship between peoples and who is shown the value of real cooperation. Or it might be a collective farm which has smashed all records in milk-production, where a milkmaid recounts the progress of socialist agriculture. Or it might be the inauguration of a memorial where a veteran recalls the heroic efforts of the Soviet people during the Great Patriotic War: or, again, somewhere an exhibition is opened and Delegate So-and-So seizes the chance to draw a picture of Soviet science and its immense contribution to world peace.

In short, there is always some ceremony the media can get their teeth into, and embellish with observations suited to the circumstances.

Under '*glasnost*' the task of the media is even easier. On the one hand the Press has to denounce the abuses and the sloppiness of local party bosses, thus helping the 'political direction', i.e. the Central Party, to reinforce the authority of the centre over the local satraps, who had got out of hand during Brezhnev's time, when the Central Party was content with a purely nominal authority. On the other hand the media must advertize the 'positive experience' of *Perestroika*, publicising the success stories about economic 'reform' so that they might be 'generalized'.

Such is the 'content' of the Soviet press: and such is the 'news' which it daily offers to its readers. The events reported are as much a part of the ritual as the language itself, and just as predictable.[8]

They are as devoid of reality as the language is devoid of thought. The events are mere representations: not even that – only representations of representations. A delegate represents those who have picked him as the Party represents the people it derives from, and as Gorbachev represents the Party. Every solemn commemoration of an historic event is already transformed into symbol and there made immortal. Likewise medals and decorations are merely emblems; the achievement of the stakhanovite or the milkmaid refers always to something other than itself.

The Soviet press creates the impression that men and things reveal themselves only in a few stable selected forms

– officially accredited forms, one could say: they are fixed to
the scenery by their delegates. When they act, individually
or collectively, they do so under the ritual guise of
achievement. Except for articles devoted to foreign policy,
which receive the particular treatment described above, and
for articles describing Party congresses and meetings, there
is no reference to current affairs. The passage of time is
marked only by anniversary celebrations: the regular
succession of these events and of the Plans which measure
time in the Socialist world contrasts with the dramatic way
the capitalist camp experiences history. In the Socialist
world there is no news, only symbols which support the
current application of the Party line. Whence the deeply felt
shock when the death of the Great Leader has to be
announced: his end is the only manifestation of the laws of
nature which cannot be concealed.

In place of the confused world of the Western media, full
of accidents and contingencies, where only the unexpected
holds the readers' attention, the Soviet press substitutes a
stage on which boring allegories take their turn at the
footlights for the length of one article. All these stakhano-
rites, veterans, milkmaids and various delegates lend their
mouth to one standardised unique speech; each in turn
becomes the temporary repository of the unchanging *langue
de bois*. Each issue of *Pravda* and *Izvestia* is embellished
with photographs of workers and farm hands. In fact, these
smiling miners and rosy-cheeked peasant girls are there to
show that Newspeak can actually be spoken by ordinary
people.

This false individualisation of people by means of
allegory is the self-disguise of ceremonial Newspeak: the
tribute it pays to reality. In this instance Newspeak
digresses from the norm represented by the leading article
on the front page: an article always intended to exemplify
pure Newspeak, and which is not assigned to any particular
speaker. The leading article will be devoted to one or other

of the most common topics of 'wooden' writing, such as the necessity of increasing and improving production, of safe-guarding peace or bringing in the harvest on time. Against a background of this dry rehearsal of the political line, the model workers and representatives of foreign 'freedom-fighters' almost come to life in the same way that against a background of stock stereotypes the reports from Afghanis-tan and the descents into the underground dens of Western anti-Communism seem to ring true.

Here, we touch on one of the secrets of the effectiveness of Newspeak, one of its essential qualities and one which shows how much the *langue de bois* is a part of ideology. There is a striking similarity between the structure of the *langue de bois* as depicted here and the well-known Communist tactic of praising the right 'line' and the 'responsible' attitude that allegedly avoids every kind of deviation. Compared with the utopian nonsense of *Prolet-kult* (a movement of the 'twenties which claimed to have created a proletarian art and which dismissed all 'bourgeois art'), the views of Lenin seem a model of moderation and rationality. In face of Trotsky's extremism one could only rejoice at Stalin's victory. The same Stalin looks like the spokesman of good sense compared with the excesses of the followers of M.J. Marr. Likewise Gorbachev appears on the stage as the quintessence of reason and commonsense against a background of neo-Stalinists *à la* Nina Andreyeva and demagogues *à la* Yeltsin.

Ideology likes to distinguish itself from extreme nihilism and from 'leftist deviators'. These frighten away reason and bring people to accept almost anything, provided it seems more moderate. Even under Stalin, people believed they had avoided the worst. When he died, they wept, fearing worse would come. The citizen of a Communist state always has the feeling that he has 'escaped the worst'. But in actuality the moderate version of ideology is no less dangerous and destructive than its extreme form: for

instance Lenin's views on art are as deadly as the nihilism of
Proletkult. We have since seen what Stalin's 'moderation'
meant. But it is accepted with relief, because of the sheer
terror inspired by the extreme version. This well-tried
technique of obfuscation is behind the myth that 'hawks'
and 'doves' are in conflict in the Kremlin, thanks to which
myth Western countries make all sorts of concessions in
order to avoid giving the advantage to the formidable
'hawks'.

This marvellously effective device is to be found in its
entirety in Newspeak. The leading article on the first page
of the newspaper presents the most extreme form of
Newspeak. That style then seems to put on a human face in
the 'news columns', which are apparently about people of
flesh and blood. Finally, Newspeak attains an almost
'normal' manner, when it describes the hidden depths of the
hostile world.

Of course the Soviet reader pays most attention to the
passages which seem to be written in an almost natural style
– that is the ones which are most ideologically offensive. In
other words Newspeak uses its extreme form to make the
reader accept, without very much resistance, and even with
relief, its 'moderate'[9] mode; which is most important from
the ideological viewpoint. This ability to modulate from
mode to mode, so essential for Newspeak's effectiveness,
distinguishes the language of wood from all other
propaganda-languages and of course from natural political
speech. Allegory and narrative seem to offer an asylum
from that chilling ceremonial Newspeak which is without
either subject or object. But as we have seen, reason is
never in such danger as in its instinctive flight towards what
looks familiar, where it ends up with both feet in the traps
of ideology.

Linguistic Hijacking

Grammar

Newspeak exploits not only reason's survival-instinct in order to capture the mind; it plays other tricks, besides that of ringing the modal changes.

The tricks are, first and foremost, linguistic. In a Communist society *langue de bois* has the monopoly of intellectual formulation, and we should not under-estimate the advantage it derives from that. In a society where so much is unsaid, what *is* said has extra weight. (In a shapeless world, even a sketchy outline is irresistible and easily holds the attention.) The techniques of suppression and illustration can destroy the intelligibility of the real. When man is reduced to those extremes the hunger for sense is so great that any structure at all, especially, a linguistic structure, can satisfy it.

Roman Jakobson has demonstrated the power of the grammatical *Gestalt* by comparing the phrase: 'Colourless green ideas sleep furiously', in which Chomsky saw non-sense, with the following non-grammatical groups of words: 'Furiously sleep ideas green colourless'[10] An 'ontological non-reality', to borrow Jakobson's term, when written in grammatically coherent language, makes sense. If there is no other rival language for comparison because of the official monopoly of language, the 'onotological non-reality' which is declared to exist can end up by ringing true.

Grammar irresistibly suggests existence. 'Even nothing-ness takes on a sort of existence when we speak of it'[11] wrote Condillac. The human mind is reluctant to admit that one can speak of nothing at all. Any proposition which is grammatically coherent is accepted. Plato concluded that non-being did exist from the fact that we could discuss it.

According to him the success of the Sophists derived precisely from their irrational refusal to admit that language could formulate non-being. Newspeak profits from the willingness of the mind to accept forms and uses its grammatical credit to the full. Newspeak has the monopoly of articulated speech and greatly benefits from it in the emantic vacuum which it unceasingly creates around itself. *Langue de bois* entices the understanding by the promise of a new intelligibility, which it highlights in language's regular constructions. It shatters the cover of linguistic rigour and substitutes the order of ideology for the real order of things. Furthermore, Newspeak discovers the technique of its own self-generation among purely linguistic mechanisms.

Figures and tropes

All language includes a series of devices for extending itself. Some enable it to express matters which for one reason or another are difficult to put into words: others enable matters to be hinted at rather than made explicit. To meet our need to express ourselves and to help fill its own gaps, language provides figures of speech and tropes. We have seen what sort of metaphors the language of Communism is ornamented with; but we must not overlook other figures of speech which throw even more light on Newspeak's functioning. For they are used in its own specifically debauched way. These figures do not embellish speech or make it more expressive, as happens in ordinary language. They are used in a devious manner characteristic of Newspeak. Far from showing an intent to extend meaning they are there to furnish Newspeak's empty spaces and to reiterate what has already been stated; and, above all, to act as a dynamo generating speech-power.

Newspeak has an obvious preference for certain figures of speech, especially allegory, personification and metonymy. These tropes are summoned up not only to catalogue good things and bad things, to 'place' them definitively or to make them play scenes on the stage of history. Beyond all that, their role is to provide themes for speech. Deprived of the function of describing reality or of embodying living thought, Newspeak sticks slavishly to effigies. There is nothing surprising in the fact that Communists see puppet figures everywhere, for as soon as they depart from the abstract all their rhetoric is arranged around arbitrary personifications. If Communist language was not towed along by figures of speech, it would collapse ignominiously on itself, a hollow thing spoken by no one and speaking of nothing.

By means of the manichean allegory, the resistance of real-life phenomena to the claims of ideology is explained away as a sort of aggregate of actions in bad faith on the part of the enemies of progress. Allegory is indeed the only resort of a language which seeks to avoid all mention of real phenomena and actual events. Allegory introduces a fictitious differentiation between opposites, thus making speech possible and giving the *langue de bois* its alibi. Thanks to allegory, language is given an object to discuss; and, eventually, a subject appears to do the talking.

Metonymy does quite as much to generate Communist language. Metonymy is frequent in all discourse. One speaks equally easily of 'the White House', 'the Kremlin', 'the Elysée'. But the essential purpose of metonymy in the Communist press is pejorative: it identifies the enemy. There are numerous references to 'the Pentagon' and 'Wall Street' but the Soviet authorities never receive such cavalier treatment. Instead of the insulting abbreviations of Western institutions and personages used by the bourgeois Press they prefer a pompous periphrasis. 'The Kremlin' is never admissible as a short-hand for the 'Party and the government, under the guidance of ... '

But metonymy does not only label enemies; it helps

Newspeak in its task of linguistic falsification. We have seen how a detail taken from its context can be integrated into an ideological structure so as to lend reality to the whole. Metonymy is the very figure of speech which effects this transfer from the part to the whole. The transfer is so natural that one forgets that the whole into which the part is verbally blended is itself pure fiction. One forgets that the association is logically illegitimate, being justified neither by a link of cause and effect, nor by a sequential link, nor through any symbolic relationship or rapport.[12] In Newspeak the metonymy is corrupted, because it is no longer used to show the relationships between things, but, on the contrary, to isolate a fact from its context and cut it off from everything that would make it intelligible. This is done in order to make the fact depend on the doctrine. The doctrine henceforth will monopolise all rights of interpretation. All information about the West is presented in the form of metonymy. However there is no real correspondence between the selected fragment and the ideological whole that it is supposed to represent. Personification makes it possible to identify the opposing forces but metonymy can do something much more useful: it can define and characterize them. Metonymy and personification provide the means by which ideology gets its purchase on the world. For they convert real-life phenomena into manageable children's building blocks or lead soldiers – alternately bogeymen and 'paper tigers'.

The use of tropes enables Newspeak to swallow even the indigestible *Solidarność*. Metonymy begins the process by reducing the organisation to KOR alone which then acts as a sort of lightning conductor to attract Soviet thunderbolts. Next KOR is boiled down to a few people like Kuroń and Michnik, who embody and personify the diabolical forces at work in Poland. Two figures of speech were enough to absorb the Polish movement into the 'universe of wood'.

However, it is the repeated and varied use of *metalepsis*

that demonstrates above all how much Newspeak depends on the driving force of language-production. Metalepsis is the figure of speech by which 'one explains what is to follow by what has gone before, or that which has gone before by that which follows'.[13] In speech it is the equivalent of implication or presupposition. A great many terms and phrases which recur in Newspeak are actually metalepses: for example, words which indicate processes – such as 'enlarging', 'enriching', 'aggravating', 'stressing' and 'emphasizing' – have meaning only in what they imply for the past and the future simultaneously: that is to say that the given phenomena have a previous existence and will grow stronger. Their terms relate at the same time to what was and what will be. The present is omitted altogether. The dynamism that they claim to pinpoint in reality is passed on to the text; or, rather, the linguistic simulation of movement is part of the production-technique of a kind of speech which is incapable of any relationship with real objects isolated in space, or with real facts existing in time. The comparative plays exactly the same role, acting as a metalepsis by expanding past processes into the future. Metalepsis is to be found also in the noun-phrases which are so characteristic of Newspeak – phrases which presume some past fact, given once for all and presented as proven. The phrase 'the correctness of Leninist theses' implies that the proposition 'Leninist theses are correct' is true.[14] This ingenious way of using metalepsis means that it is impossible to rebut any 'wooden' statement without making a concession which annihilates the rebuttal. Thus, the defendant, when he desperately pleads: 'I have never been part of the criminal plans of Tito and his clique', concedes the essential fact. He acknowledges that Tito did in fact devise such plans.[15] There are not many people who can contend simultaneously with words and their implications. Newspeak does not allow one to say what one wants. Once one accepts the allegorical idiom, one allows the words to be put in one's mouth.

Metalepsis is par excellence the figure of speech of the creative verb. According to Fontanier, it can be likened to 'the device by which a poet or writer claims, or is claimed, to invent by himself that which he in fact only narrates or describes', and that other device by which 'the writer suddenly abandons the role of narrator for that of master and sovereign; and instead of simply telling of things in process of happening or already done, he commands and orders that they should be created'.[16] This stealthy modulation from apparent narration to the conjuring up of reality is a feature of ideological texts. The principle which underlies two extreme modes of metalepsis, as defined by Fontanier, is the very principle which informs the *langue de bois* and socialist realism, except that the speaker or author is in most cases undetectable. For this reason the figure of speech escapes detection.

Ordinary language uses figures of speech to make up for its inadequacies. The various tropes are exceptional devices which enable it to express and communicate an original idea, a strong emotion or some novel concept. In other words, they enable the text to live up to its subject. In Newspeak tropes are also used to draw out and prolong language. But here there is no question of seeking a greater equivalence between words and thought. In Newspeak language is stretched in order to conceal the nothingness which threatens all the time to show through. By packing itself with tropes, Newspeak avoids shipwreck in the sea of its own emptiness. That is why the tropes are kept out of sight: for it is essential to hide the fact that this language is sustained by nothing more than itself; that it is kept going only by its own mess. Figures of speech have one more advantage – more than grammar, they can suggest an urgent, imminent meaning and can defer a total understanding to the past or to the future, and so make people believe vaguely in these elusive abstractions that would otherwise be unintelligible.

Tautology

Newspeak does not always misuse language in so subtle a fashion. Language can be stretched, but more easily still it can be repeated. Communist pen-pushers have never shunned repetition, which acts as an effective soporific, inducing an appropriate torpor in the mind. Tautology is a kind of incantation designed to accompany the emergence of Truth. It can create a hypnotic state in which human beings lose all sense of reality. Lenin was a grand master in the use of tautology, as we can see from a speech he made in 1920 to the Third Congress of the Komsomol:

> We reject all morality which has not a human, class perspective. We affirm that it is a fraud, a deceit and a form of brain-washing imposed on workers and peasants in the interest of plutocrats and capitalists. We declare that our morality is entirely subordinate to the interests of the working class in its struggle. Our morality is dedicated to the benefit of the class war ...
>
> And this is why we say so: for us, morality detached from human society has no existence: it is a fraud. For us, morality is subordinate to the proletariat's class struggle.

Repetition here is more than a pedagogic process. Stylistically it incarnates the invincible clarity and supreme authority of the idea. More remarkable still, tautology is hidden behind a pseudo-logical progression created by the words: 'And this is why'. The language simulates logical progressions and developments of thought while remaining completely motionless and reduced to an echo of itself. Henri Barbusse constantly uses false thought-processes

(chains of reasoning) and unblushingly produces statements
like this –

> To put a work into the right place, one must follow the
> direction it has taken and its points of departure and then
> enrich its basic arguments again before starting once more.[17]

Constant in all communist writing are references to
'clarity', 'coherence' (G. Marchais: 'This programme offers
a clear and coherent view of a profound change'[18]) and
'logic', as if the mere sounding of these words were
sufficient proof of live thought. The chains of reasoning
never seem stronger than when they encompass absolutely
nothing. The 'bronze fetters' of Newspeak contain nothing
more than tautology.

So, under cover of Newspeak, ideology eliminates the
order of nature and puts in its place a series of abstractions
emanating from an understanding which, because the
sounding of vocables always seems to denote the existence
of live thought, remains unaware of its own paralysis. One
comes to understand why ideology is sometimes difficult to
spot: the reason is that it works with the help of invisible
linguistic devices and uses words which create an appearance of rationality. This makes ideology's position almost
impregnable. It seems accountable to reason, because of its
unbreakable network of grammatical links, its impenetrable
panoply of figures of speech. As its mechanisms operate
beyond the realm of consciousness, ideology is in little
danger of being flushed out by reason: for it lies where no
one would dream of looking.

As between things and words, the human understanding
will always choose words which are its own special tools and
which always deliver meaning without being asked. Ideology is seductive because it invites the understanding to
regard things as if they *were* words, that is, as signs which

vanish after use. Ideology turns the world into language. Reality then becomes as permeable to the mind as language is; and as ephemeral. Moreover it is always easier to pile up phrases than to grasp ideas. Newspeak resolves the double difficulty of understanding things and expressing that understanding, by replacing phenomena and events by tropes, and reasoning by tautology. Thus the temptation to rely too much on words becomes almost irresistible: by parodying the sense of reality and of intellectual rigour, Newspeak simultaneously attacks the two elements that would help the mind to resist it. 'Men's opinions take a strange path once abstractions, metaphors, metonymies and other tropes are seen as really existent, are used as principles and the basis of reasoning'.[19] In a society where only one mode of speech is allowed, the danger foreseen by Président de Brosses becomes lethal. Because it is accustomed to work in a vacuum, reason turns away from the harsh reality-principle, preferring well-trodden pathways where words function merely as illuminated signposts.

Newspeak operates by means of a double deceit: it dissociates words and things and then pretends to make up for the absence of meaning by sketching an alternative universe. This universe is completely and immediately meaningful, because it happens to be structured like language. This thoroughly intelligible world makes one forget that the words which describe it are meaningless and that the objects which furnish it do not exist. Reason is no sooner called into play than it is, inevitably, neutralized.

HOW LANGUE DE BOIS *PARALYSES REASON*

Not only does Newspeak force the mind to go round in circles (while maintaining an illusion of logical progression). Not only does it corrupt the understanding by making everything seem easy, it undertakes as well the difficult task of assimilating the stubborn facts of reality without providing any new food for thought.

The dialectic

This amazing feat is made possible by the manichean nature of ideology. All Newspeak has to do is to translate into words the foreknowledge implicit in the total manichean vision; it may then make use of the consequent duality. By means of this oblique device, novelties can be absorbed into the old dual conception and unforeseen elements, which for one reason or another cannot be concealed, can be integrated into the ideology. This is the function of wooden dialectic, which consists of shaking off unwanted facts at the end of a cunning procedure.

The manichean vision derives from the fundamental opposition between 'progressive' and 'reactionary'. From this essential opposition springs a whole series of antithetic concepts upon which Newspeak projects anything that it wishes to destroy. By the end of this 'shuttle', one loses sight of the object without realizing it. These opposed pairs, whose range of deployment is of great tactical interest, are generally lined up as follows: 'form' is opposed to 'content', 'abstract' to 'concrete', 'objective' to 'subjective', 'whole' to 'part', 'reflection' to 'interests' and 'true nature' to 'appearance'. The pairs in a way represent the upper and lower jaws of ideology.

The following examples, taken from the Soviet press, illustrate the way this marvellous apparatus works. The revolution in Iran presented a serious problem: it was a true revolution, but it was a religious one. Thanks to dialectic, this obstacle was overcome quite easily and the Iranian event made to fit nicely into the ideological 'pattern'. This was done simply by using the opposition between 'form' and 'content'. At the end of this 'creative analysis' it was then possible to say that the Iranian revolution was effectively progressive, since it was religious only in form. Its content obviously revealed the class struggle. The form carries away what is ideologically undesirable while the content gives the essential.

Are there still shortages within the Soviet economy? Such defects occur only in certain sectors: the whole remains healthy and satisfactory ('globally positive' in the words of Georges Marchais). And so the disastrous situation in agriculture and the formidable chronic deficits are brushed aside ... Do Bourgeois scientists maintain that the U.S.S.R. is plagued by pollution? Their statements stick too narrowly to the concrete. They should adopt a more abstract and general point of view and understand that, as long as the means of production belong to the people, there cannot be abuses similar to those caused by capitalist sharks. Do collective farms function badly, as one hears? Barbusse explains:

Collective farms, like Soviets, represent only the form of socialist organisation ... but the form only. Everything depends on the content.[20]

As for Trotsky, predilection for the part to the detriment of the whole makes him a schismatic:

His critical sense was excessive and without breadth ... his concentration on detail prevented him from looking at the whole.[21]

Thus stubborn facts disappear one after the other through the great trapdoor of ideology. The principal quality of a communist theorist is his skill in handling these magic pairs, these jaws capable of grinding anything. Once he has mastered the dialectic, the theorist is equipped with a 'creative approach' to phenomena. He will know how to place things in their context, that is, how to pass from the concrete to the abstract and vice versa: he will know how to interpret the part in the light of the whole and how to refute appearances. Thanks to dialectic, Newspeak is never short of devices and ideology never at a loss.

For several reasons dialectic has a devastating effect on the mind. First, it pre-supposes intellectual dishonesty. There is, however, more than the moral corruption of the intelligent. Dialectic enables the *langue de bois* to mimic the work of the mind: to ape the process of understanding and to create the illusion of mental activity, by using terms which suggest an act of comprehension. The reader really thinks he is moving from the concrete to the abstract, from appearances to a real essence, from an unimportant detail to what is essential because that is what the words suggest. In fact, lulled by these glib assurances, thought is at a standstill without the thinker realizing it. Communist power has understood that in order to get rid of an undesirable object, it is better to counterfeit it rather than simply to suppress it. For the copy destroys the real object more surely than physical demolition could. So communism creates sham laws, sham religion and sham culture, as Alexander Zinoviev has convincingly shown. This is also true of the dialectic itself, which is nothing but an imitation of true thought.

The third danger which arises from dialectic is that it suppresses the object to which the mind should be attending, replacing it by a process of oscillation between imaginary concepts. Instead of being fed from outside, the mind has to feed on itself and to sustain itself solely with its own products. For ideological thought moves in a closed circuit and it is the *langue de bois* which starts it up again and again. Dialectic isolates the understanding from anything which could help it to break out of itself.

The dialectical process is, one may say, a model of Newspeak, its weapon and a clue to its true nature. At the very moment when reason is seduced by the promise of total triumph in which no phenomenon will be able to escape the interpretation prepared for it, the mind dwindles from lack of nourishment. The fundamental role of the dialectic in Newspeak is not solely to implant conviction, but to destroy the mind itself.

Pathos

The 'scientoidal' style and pathos both work in the same direction. Newspeak plays on these two registers for the same reason that it turns to dialectic: to frustrate the understanding whilst corrupting it by an illusion of all embracing knowledge. At the moment when Truth reveals itself, emotion gains the upper hand and hinders all judgment. The presence of Truth is accepted not because ideological statements are verified but because the linguistic style indicates the emotion which should arise from the emergence of genuine truth. But Truth cannot be soberly examined, since the language precludes any possibility of dispassionate enquiry. Once more Barbusse puts it admirably: ' *One must* acknowledge all these phenomena *with emotion*, if one wishes to remain objective.'[22] About collectivisation, he states: 'The *rationality* of this organisation of agriculture (...) so revealed to us only through its most *touching* statistics.' [23]

At the very moment when total intelligibility seems imminent, reason is sent packing. Emotion has intervened to prevent reason from examining the validity of the arguments which are thrust at it.

Such is the circle in which *langue de bois* traps its victims: reason calls up emotions which operate against reason; hence they neutralize each other. The result is that ideological speech does not aim to build up a conviction based on the assent of heart and mind. It seeks rather to corrupt the operations of all our mental faculties, by setting them against each other, by corrupting one faculty by another, and by confusing them with periodical bursts of emotion. The mind cannot function unless it enjoys a certain continuity. Newspeak attacks continuity in two ways. It destroys the links between phenomena; it rations the time which the mind needs for thought. So thought is, in effect, suspended by pathos, which itself soon turns into an urge to act. Then the need for adequate interpretation surfaces again, and this restarts the cycle. Pathos acts as an artificial dynamo which prevents the mind from turning inwards and becoming conscious of itself. The stylistic peculiarities of Newspeak stem from this will to foster instability and to guarantee 'the banishment of reality.'[24]

So reason finds itself continually prey to exhaustion and

giddiness. The dialectic attacks it with a 'scorched earth' tactic, while tautology keep it spinning around indefinitely. Emotionalism interrupts and harries it. Newspeak is not only void of thought, it is at war with it. We have to ask, therefore, whether this assemblage of words, hostile both to reality and to the mind, is a true language at all and, if not, what its relationship is to ordinary language.

NEWSPEAK AND ORDINARY LANGUAGE

Liberty and constraint in Newspeak and in natural language

All speech is a compromise between the wish for individual expression and the established norms of linguistic usage. Jakobson refers to 'an ascending scale of freedom in combining linguistic units'. Totally absent in the combination of distinctive features into phonemes, barely existent in the grouping of phonemes into words, the freedom of the speaker increases when it comes to his grouping words to form a phrase; and it becomes complete in his arrangement of phrases in a statement.

For every linguistic sign, Jakobson distinguishes two kinds of arrangement; combination and selection (that is to say, the possibility of substituting one term for another).[25] According to Jakobson 'the restraining power of the grammatical structure (...) contrasts with the relative liberty which exists in the choice of words.' This observation obviously does not apply to Newspeak where groups of words are often of enormous length, each word ineluctably attracting another, and each phrase often dragging in another phrase. Thus freedom to combine is not only restricted by the constraints of phonology and syntax, it is also limited at the level of the phrase and even the sentence.

In Newspeak there is almost no freedom of substitution.

In Newspeak the speaker, if there is one, makes no effort to shape his thought, being content to let Newspeak speak through him at specific moments in his social existence. The speaker who uses ordinary language tries to make his words express, as well as they can, the thoughts which form in his mind. Language is built up in two stages: ' the devising of the sign which groups and conveys the thought is the *second* stage of a phenomenon of which language is the outcome: the *first* stage is the creation of the meaning, whose vehicle the sign once devised will become.'[26]

Neither of these stages occurs in Newspeak, where, if it is to work, speech must conform not to an idea but to a linguistic model – Newspeak always leans towards quotation. Unlike ordinary language, *langue de bois* expresses neither facts nor opinions. On the contrary, it tries to suppress what actually exists and to summon up what ought to be. It very much resembles magical incantation and that is why it loses its power when it departs even from the canonical formulae. To be fully effective, it has to be totally ritualistic.

Functions of language and how they work

It is interesting to consider how a language, whose great virtue is its fidelity to a model text, differs from a language which, in principle, is intended actually to say something. Jakobson[27] has identified six factors of linguistical communication which define the functions of language. These six factors are the referent, or context (i.e. what is referred to), the addresser (the speaker), the addressee (the person spoken to), the message (what is said), the code (the system of signs common to addresser and addressee) and the contact (that which enables the two to establish and

maintain communication). Each of these factors defines a
different linguistic function. Thus we have the functions of
reference, of expression, of exhortation, the poetic, the
metalinguistic and the phatic. A statement will usually fulfil
several of these functions at the same time, but one of them
will always predominate.

How are these functions exercised in Communist
discourse?[28] And how do the six factors defined by
Jakobson present themselves?

In Newspeak the addresser is seldom specified: even
when he is named, he is personally irrelevant, because he
speaks as a representative of the Party, the Government
and finally of the people. No addresser opts for Newspeak
and there is no need for him to do so since Newspeak
merely reproduces a previous statement. Newspeak rules
out all subjects just as it avoids verbs.

The addressee is as vague as the addresser. Often the two
blend with each other. In effect, *langue de bois* is addressed
to the people, and ultimately to all progressive humanity.
Unlike the addresser, however, the addressee is rarely
personified, except in the course of a diplomatic exchange.

The referent of Newspeak is Newspeak. Any excursions
beyond its boundaries would destroy the idiom itself.
Ordinary language is an open system because it has to face
up to an infinite variety of thoughts and situations.
Newspeak is a closed one because it aims to refer everything
back to some previous statement. In Jakobson's terminology that amounts to saying that the referent, the message and
the code are merged. The message is no more than a pretext
for restating the code and the referent, the two being
identical. Or to put it perhaps more accurately, in Newspeak there is no message – the code makes that an
impossibility. This explains why censorship becomes almost
superfluous in Communist countries: it is replaced by
editing.

The factor of 'contact' is very important in Newspeak; its

peculiar character derives from the specific role played by language in Communist society. The following chapter will deal with this fundamental issue.

Of the six factors of verbal communication, two clearly persist in *langue de bois*: the code and the contact. One can therefore expect the functions of metalanguage and contact to predominate.

Metalanguage occurs each time that 'discourse centres on the code'. In ordinary language this happens every time speakers wish to make sure that they are using the same language, or that they attribute the same meanings to the same words. Metalanguage plays an important part in linguistic learning, especially among children, according to Jakobson. Nevertheless in normal cases such a function is secondary. In Newspeak, however, metalanguage becomes of prime importance since the code serves both as an expression of power and as a   sign of submission to power.

The preponderance of the metalinguistic function accounts also for the tautological and pedagogical aspects so characteristic of Newspeak. Ideological speech heaps up definitions because it has no other way of imposing its polarised code: in this regard our quotations from Lenin are typical. He who expresses himself in Newspeak is incapable of formulating a synthetic proposition: he has to content himself with parading analytical judgements. He does not know that he is doing so, however, since he is also expressing value-judgements at the same time. Wooden metalanguage conveys nothing about concepts: it simply surrounds them with sign words of approval or disapproval. Wooden definitions are nothing more than polarized tautologies; they belong exclusively to metalanguage, since they invariably concern the determination of the code and the fixing of its application.

The importance of the metalinguistic function shows how closely Newspeak is linked to power. For it is power that has the permanent role of making adjustments to the code.

It is power also which has to make sure that its subjects continuously adhere to whatever the Party line is. By promoting the function of metalanguage within language, the Communist regime has learned how to concentrate maximum power within society; whenever he utters Newspeak, a citizen shows his own submission. At the same time, however, he spreads the power of the ideology and gains authority himself in proportion to his own docility. Power is both affirmed and passed on in the same action.

The metalinguistic function involves in turn the phatic function – that is, messages which 'make sure that the circuit is operating, attract the listener's attention or make sure that it does not wander' by promoting 'a lavish exchange of stylized formulas'.[29] Obviously this phatic function plays a great part in Newspeak. It is not, however, a matter of making simple contact and sustaining it, as is the case in ordinary language. The contact to be created and preserved is that of power and the 'stylized formulas' are chosen by authority itself. Even more important is the need to guarantee that the ideological circuit is unbroken and that contact with doctrine is not interrupted even for a moment. The phatic function lies at the bottom of the incantation: for whoever wishes to summon up magic forces and enter into communion with them makes use of ritualised phrases. In the same fashion, Newspeak summons up what *must* be, striving, as it were, to keep abreast of the future.

This orientation towards a power which encompasses both present people and future things, explains why ideological speech is dominated by an alliance of the metalinguistic and phatic functions. Incidentally, it also explains one of Newspeak's most striking characteristics: the co-existence of extreme arbitrariness and extreme ritualism. Both arise from the same desire for absolute power and the same need to demonstrate the presence of that power. Together they ruin language completely.

Arbitrariness cuts off words from their ordinary meanings and injects them with this content or that at the whim of the authorities; while, because of ritualism, words can no longer be freely combined into phrases but must march solemnly in pre-arranged formations. The predominance of the metalinguistic and social functions simply turns language upside down. Where ordinary language is freedom, *langue de bois* is nothing but constraint. Where ordinary, natural language rests on a convention, i.e. on the indispensable bond between the signifier and the signified – *langue de bois* claims complete licence.

We have still to consider what happens to the other functions of language. Ideological language claims to transmit knowledge; therefore one might expect the referential function to be equally important. In fact, the referential function is constantly absorbed by the hortatory function: narrative and description inevitably develop into command and exhortation.

The same can be said of the expressive function, already greatly compromised by the absence of an addresser. It is in fact completely overwhelmed by the hortatory function, because the emotions signalled by order from above must be felt below. The expressive function also plays a part in neutralizing the referential function – we have shown how pathos intervenes to suspend judgement. However the hortatory function which seems to be so important in Newspeak merely camouflages the overall presence of the phatic function. Commands are given to no-one in particular: they are indeed very much like incantations. In Newspeak there is no poetic function to speak of, because there is no personal creation. Even slogans hardly require verbal novelty, not at least under mature socialism. Perhaps the need to create the referent exhausts the faculty of poetic invention: and when words do not have to compete with real-life things, they do not need any ornaments.

Newspeak and meaning

Newspeak distinguishes itself from natural language by a hypertrophy of the code. This reveals the determining influence of political power on the language and its wish to dominate by magic. The code is both flexible and rigid: it lays down the verbal ceremonial, but can be altered by official decision. This hypertrophy arose through a covert transformation of signs into signals. Words in Newspeak aim, primarily, to affect behaviour; they must stimulate action. As Dr Goebbels, said 'We do not speak in order to say something, but so as to produce a particular effect.' Newspeak does not belong in the realm of semantics; and from this viewpoint we can compare it with systems of communication in the animal world. Certain sounds, such as 'revisionist', 'enemy of the people', signal the quarry; others, like 'mistake', 'lack of vigilance', serve as warnings or threats and also indicate submission. *Langue de bois* rests on a mechanism which is also to be found in natural speech, but at an infra-semantic level: study of the vocabulary shows that a large number of single words function only as one of an opposed pair, rather as the binary opposition of distinctive features enable us to define a phoneme. In wooden language, the code governs the management of the words in the same way that it dictates the combination of distinctive features in ordinary language. This confirms what has already been said about tropes: Newspeak derives the principles of its own production from the structures of language itself; it is not organized around the quest for meaning, but arises out of the subconscious reflexes which make up the language-code.

Newspeak is composed entirely of elements borrowed from ordinary language. It owes everything, words and grammar, to that source; and yet Newspeak has undergone a monstrous change and radically differs from ordinary language. It refers only to a rudimentary more or less black and white, semantic world. Not only does it empty words of their context, it also tries to deprive language of the very ability to represent anything.

In Newspeak all the elements of ordinary or natural language which enable us to place something in space or time are either suppressed or corrupted. The treatment of pronouns, adverbs of place and verbs is evidence of this. However, the manichean viewpoint does not in itself prevent verbal indications of space and time: it is the ideology's dynamic view into which manicheanism is integrated that makes such indications impossible. Abstractions conveyed by Newspeak are not the stable clearly-outlined abstractions we call concepts. They are disembodied processes whose only characteristic is *movement*. The mind cannot grasp them because nothing about them is fixed. All those 'enrichings', 'deepenings', 'enlargings', 'developments', etc. elude any kind of genuine representation. They enable Newspeak to operate with elements taken from ordinary language while avoiding the meanings which underlie it. This 'pan-dynamism' – the sensation of constant movement produced by comparatives and by similar expressions evolving the necessary, precipitate crash towards the future – causes a sort of vertigo which obscures the utter emptiness of the words. The process of subverting sense takes place in two stages: first the words are detached from their referents by means of the manichean duality; then they are swept so strongly into the overall dynamic rush that their loss of shape is hidden by the movement. The same drive to de-stabilize has already been exhibited in the style.

Newspeak preserves some of the grammar and vocabulary of ordinary language, but it obstinately rejects the distinction between subject and object; it is reluctant to use verbs and it is constantly determined to destroy meaning by removing the autonomy of all those concepts which it hurls into 'the course of history'. All this makes one wonder whether Newspeak is really a language at all.

According to G. Guillaume, 'language, however primitive it may be, demonstrates by its very existence its aim to comprehend all that can be thought about'.[30] Newspeak makes the same claim, but one can legitimately ask what thought can rely on when all external reality is removed, when thought is imprisoned in a cyclical movement which leads nowhere; when thought is deprived of fixed forms or clear abstractions; when the signs it uses lack meaning and when references to space and time are deleted. As Paul Valéry wrote: 'The true meaning of a word is to be found in what it points to outside language.'[31] Later, he added 'The role of language is essential, but with language one is in transit. One cannot settle on there.'[32] *Langue de bois* on the other hand is not transition: it does not pass into meaning like ordinary language. Its words lead to nothing but themselves. As it is, an exercise in verbalism rather than a system of meaningful signs, it cannot be understood, but only diagnosed. Unlike ordinary language which is capable of limitless extension and ever new combinations, Newspeak is narrowly constrained and its potential very restricted, despite its automatic production. To interpret it one considers less what it says than the choice it makes between the options which the code provides. Thus, when an editorial appeals for greater ideological vigilance rather than a speeding-up of production, one can be sure that certain steps will be taken to educate the citizens and strengthen their discipline. The content of the editorial matters less than the fact that a given topic has been selected. The only real bond between Newspeak and reality is its link with *power*; and the only real information it provides concerns the dispositions of that power. Newspeak is useless at presenting facts and thoughts, but it manages marvellously to fulfil its sole function: namely, to indicate the Party-line.

Notes to Chapter II

[1] Plato, *Sophist*, 252c. Eurycles was a ventriloquist.

[2] Under Gorbachevian *glasnost*, some accidents are mentioned in the media, especially when an educational purpose can be served; such as the lessons to be drawn regarding slovenly bureaucratic reaction to catastrophes and the criminal indifference of the local leaders.

[3] In this connexion see *Literaturnaya Gazeta*, 4 April 1982. Some Soviet citizens have confirmed to me that the manoeuvre was entirely successful.

[4] St Augustine, '*De mendacio*', *Oeuvres* II, *Problèmes moraux*, Paris, 1937, p. 239.

[5] The term comes from A. Besançon: '*La conviction idéologique*' in: *Commentaire*, no. 11, Autumn 1980, pp. 380-381.

[6] Gorbachev's real innovations consist above all in using this pseudo-natural language more systematically and with greater awareness.

[7] For an analysis of the techniques of falsification one can turn to an article by I.I. Levin, '*O semiotike iskazheniya istiny*' in: *Informatsionnyje voprosy semiotiki, lingvistiki i avtomaticheskogo perevoda, Vypusk 4*, Moscow, 1974.

[8] In *Les Carnets d'un badaud*, the writer Victor Nekrasov describes an unusual wager he made with students of the University of Geneva. He undertook to describe in advance the contents of an issue of *Pravda* that a student was about to fetch from the nearest kiosk. He won his bet, getting it almost exactly right. V. Nekrasov, *Les Carnet d'un badaud*, Paris, 1976

[9] It would be fascinating to study the Polish press before and after December 1981 to get an impression of the elasticity of the language of wood. In a weekly like *Tu i teraz* ('Here and Now') great concessions are made to ordinary language; but the underlying urge to promote ideology is only more obvious, and the language of wood shows through every line. In this connexion see an article by Marian Goveyki: '*W zgielko dreczonych wyrazów*' in *Wezwanie*, no. 4, 1982, pp. 280 - 35.

[10] R. Jakobson, 1963, p. 204

[11] Condillac, *Grammaire*, I, 12, Paris 1796

[12] V. du Marsais, *Traité des tropes*, Paris, 1977 and Fontanier, *Les figures du discours*, Paris, 1968.

[13] Du Marsais, 1977, p. 80.

[14] For the use of 'nominalisation' in *lingua sovietica*, see the works of P. Seriot, especially 'L.I. Brezhnev and speech about science' in: *Essais sur le discours soviétique*, Université de Grenoble III, 1981, pp. 11-63.

[15] The example is taken from the work of O. Reboul, *Langage et idéologie*, PUF, 1980. This work contains a great many acute observations and just remarks, although the author's rather hazy notions of ideology itself are open to criticism.

[16] Fontanier, 1968, p. 29

[17] H. Barbusse, 1935, p. 256.

[18] G. Marchais, 1972, p. 7.

[19] Président de Brosses, *Traité de la formation mécanique des langues et des principes de l'étymologie*, Paris, 1765, p. 289

[20] H. Barbusse, 1935, p. 258.

[21] Ibid, p. 192.

[22] Ibid, p. 119

[23] Ibid, p. 251.

[24] The phrase comes from Julien Benda. See Julien Benda, *La Trahison des Clercs*, 1977, p. 106.

[25] R. Jakobson, 1963, p. 206

[26] G. Guillaume, *Langage et science du langage*, Paris, 1964, p. 241

[27] See R. Jakobson, 1963, t.I, pp. 211 et seq.

[28] See O. Reboul, 1980. This book is almost entirely devoted to a study of the different functions of language in ideological speech. Thanks to this approach, the author has gone beyond mere analysis of the lexicon of ideological language to which researchers usual confine their attention.

[29] R. Jakobson, 1963, t.I, p. 217.

[30] G. Guillaume, 1964, p. 240

[31] P. Valéry, 1973, I, p. 456

[32] Ibid, p. 474

III

THE ROLE OF NEWSPEAK

... Language is simply the equivalent of everything which impinges on our sensibility ... one of the most grievous consequences of deceitful language is that it concentrates and even destroys that sensibility which can be seen as the soul and the strength of society ...

... To misuse language is to commit a real crime against man ...

... To misuse language is to work to destroy language itself, to make it meaningless or dangerous to society ...

... To misuse language is at once to destroy our means of communication and to undermine the foundations of our conventions. It is, without doubt, the most wicked act man can perpetrate on society ...

Fouquet d'Auxonne

Statement on the question put by the Royal Academy of Science and Literature of Prussia: Is it useful to deceive the people, either by introducing them to error, or by imprisoning them in the error they already have?

Once the specific functioning of Newspeak has been made clear – its constant playing on two opposed yet complementary modes, namely ceremonial newspeak and the pseudo-ordinary language (polemical Newspeak) – it becomes impossible to define *langue de bois* as a propaganda language, in the normal sense of the term. The polemical mode denies access to the truth, it puts reality out of reach of the mind, while the ceremonial mode provides a code. This code, unlike rhetoric, makes no attempt to persuade an audience by its eloquence. A language which holds both reality and the human soul in contempt has nothing in common with normal propaganda. Nor is lying its primary role. Lying occurs only exceptionally, when Newspeak seeks to brush aside some reality which threatens the closed circle of ceremonial speech. Yet this special language plays a crucial role in the Communist state. This is shown, for one thing, by its extraordinary prolixity. Newspeak's role is difficult to grasp because it is so hard to imagine what use there can be in a language that is cut off from meaning. Thus the Western mind persists in associating Newspeak in one way or another with meaning and in seeing it as a kind of political language. Actually, its usefulness is of a quite different order.

LANGUAGE AND IDEOLOGY: MARR AND STALIN

Let us approach the problem from a different angle. It may be useful to follow Alexander Zinoviev's advice and examine the status allotted to this language within the official ideology. The more so because there we can make use of a document of great prestige. For Stalin himself condescended to take an interest in linguistics and wrote a personal refutation of the man who was then the highest authority in Soviet linguistic science, N.J. Marr. Why did Marr's theories displease Stalin?

As a naive beginner in Marxism, Marr taught that language was part of the 'superstructure' and closely dependent on its base. Just as society had progressed through various stages, so language had passed through phases of development too. Starting as gestures, language had become oral speech with the development of production relations. After the proletariat's victory language would disappear, since the triumph of the workers would be the triumph also of pure thought. The classless society would be endowed with a new kind of language which would not consist of gestures or spoken words. This new language would display the 'triumph of thought over language'. Marr never took the risk of stating precisely what the characteristics of this new language would be. In his own words:

> Our final victory, as demanded by the proletariat, is the fusion of science and its ideological technique with art and its formal technique, together with the union of beauty and the intelligence in dialectical, materialistic, proletarian thought. Dialectical-materialist thought has no successor but is itself without limits; for it contains within itself boundless possibilities of growth; in width and depth, in space and time. Language has settled with some difficulty for the time being on the spoken word and is preparing to leave the latter behind and to create, on the basis of its final achievements, a new unique language which will merge supreme beauty with the highest development of the intelligence. Where will this happen? Comrades, it can happen only in Communist society, in a society without classes.
>
> Formal logic, the legacy of class thought and the class which created it, will be replaced by the dialectical-materialist thought of the proletariat and the ideologico-technological world view. There thought prevails, and will prevail more and more over language until not only will spoken language disappear from the classless society but a unique language will be created which will differ more from oral language than oral language differs from gesture language. There will be a new instrument of production too, which will endow humanity with a unique way of thinking as well as with a unique language which will make man master of all places and all times.[1]

Further on, Marr gives a definition of the universal language which is to come: a remarkable definition, because it shows with rare clarity the two fundamental characteristics of ideology, hatred of nature and rejection of all mediation. 'The language of the future is the thought that develops in the technique which is freed from the material world. No language will be able to withstand it, not even the spoken one, which is after all still bonded to the natural world.'[2]

In his many works, Marr takes great trouble to show that all languages converge towards a single language. His pet hates are, obviously, the Western linguists, with their reactionary attachment to the theory of Indo-European roots. According to Marr, it is ridiculous to imagine that modern languages in all their diversity are derived from a single idiom, since the movement of history proceeds clearly from the Many to the One. Marr's style is also worth noting. The extracts give some idea of it. One gains the impression that Marr is seeking absolution for his relatively late conversion to Marxism by a formidable display of Newspeak. The concepts of Newspeak are piled on each other in total disorder. His frantic desire to show off his missionary zeal makes his writings look like a Madame Tussaud of *langue de bois*. Marr, one may say, is a representative of the baroque age of the *lingua sovietica*.

When Stalin intervened to silence the ravings of Marr and his disciples (who indeed had had enough time to destroy Soviet linguistics) – he played once more his favourite role of champion of good sense and moderation. His short treatise *Marxism and the Linguistics Question* contains a detailed critique of Marr's propositions. It is absurd, argues Stalin, to regard language as a superstructure which must be completely reformed every time there is a change in the basis of society. For language is an instrument which, like a machine, can be exploited equally well by capitalism or by socialism. The Russian language had rendered great services to the old system; it could serve the new regime just as well. So there was absolutely no need to change its structure because of its new purpose.

The old social structure can and must be destroyed and replaced by a new one in a few years' time, so as to make room for the development of the productive forces of society. How, though, are we to annihilate the existing language and replace it in a few years with another one without sowing the seeds of anarchy and risking the collapse of society? Who, indeed, but a few Don Quixotes, would want to try?[3]

In 1952, Stalin showed himself very sceptical about the idea of a universal language which he had defended in 1930.[4] This however is not the element in Marr's teaching which triggered off Stalin's main criticism. The eccentricities of the New Theory of language could scarcely shock a man who had accepted Lysenko, whose biological fantasies had far more sinister consequences for the country. One should, then, not be deceived by the apparent moderation which Stalin affected: he opposed Marr from the strict viewpoint of an ideologue.

At the outset, Marr had made a mistake which was common to many 'intellectuals' in the 'twenties: like the *Proletkult* and *Trotsky*, he indulged in too much candour. Marr had all the attributes of an ideologue except one - the will to conceal. He displayed his devotion to ideology with a simple untreated Newspeak, and the most lyrical Marxism. But he was one who because of his extreme enthusiasm risked giving the game away by showing the nothingness of ideology.

After all, from a certain point of view, Marr was dangerously close to the truth. Communist society had indeed engendered a new universal language, detached from nature and subordinate to pure thought. In his writings, Marr had naively announced the coming of Newspeak and, through his purely negative definitions, had given more than a glimpse of the future inanity of that unique language. Even an intuition of the truth, however obscure and contorted, puts ideology at risk. Stalin knew instinctively that he must at all costs conceal the esoteric change which was taking place in the Russian language. That is why he so often stressed that Russian had hardly changed since the Revolution, except for some new words.

For Stalin, Marr's second mistake was to root language in society by considering it as part of the 'superstructure', and therefore dependent (according to Marxist theory) upon the 'base'. This idea that language is tightly linked to society Stalin found highly obnoxious; understandably he opposed it with his view of a language as a tool. However, as Benveniste shrewdly remarks:

> The description of language as a tool ... must fill us with misgiving, like every simplistic notion in linguistics. A reference to tools or instruments is a reference to the dichotomy between man and nature. The pickaxe, the arrow, the wheel are not part of nature: they are artefacts. Language is part of human nature and is not made by man ... All the characteristics of language – its immaterial nature, its symbolic functioning, its articulation, the fact that it has a content – these are enough to cast doubt on the comparison with a tool, a comparison which tends to separate man from the realm of language.[5]

There could be no better commentary on Stalin's views on the linguistic question. Nothing is to be got out of a language anchored firmly to its base, society, and locked into a superstructure which is slow to change. On the other hand language as a tool, subordinate to the will, offers infinite possibilities. All that is needed is to seize it and monopolise it. Stalin also criticized Marr for having separated thought from language and thereby having 'fallen into the swamp of idealism'. For Stalin, to assert the close bonds between thought and language was to emphasize the privileged role played by language in the propagation of ideology.[6]

In this way, under the pretext of championing common sense, Stalin seizes the opportunity to assert his own ideological voluntarism in the field of language – showing once more how his ostensibly middle position really represents a vast exercise in revolutionary demolition. By refuting Marr, Stalin is doing no other than proclaiming his own grip on language and the subordination of language to ideology.

NEWSPEAK AND POWER

As a pure artefact, Newspeak exists simply as a vehicle of power. Against Marr, Stalin defended the role of language as a mediating factor, because he needed it badly as an alternative to a situation in which power would be localised in political institutions. Power, to be total, must not be locatable in society; it must avoid clear-cut shape, it must be indivisible, impersonal and all pervasive. Communist society owes this all-pervasive and all-evasive power directly to the *langue de bois*. As long as Newspeak is assessed purely semantically, its role remains unclear; but if one views it in relation to the distribution of power within a totalitarian society, its true function becomes obvious. In actuality Newspeak does not legitimize power: it serves to spread it through society, and so becomes part of the functioning of the Communist state. Thanks to Newspeak, power, supported by ideology, seeps through the whole of the social body. Let us now consider how Newspeak fits ideology, power and society together; for in this lies one of the characteristics of the totalitarian world.

Ideology holds a potential for sheer destruction and this is seen by the people. Newspeak transmutes ideology into power in two ways. First, it formulates ideology, that is, controls and directs it. Second, it seems to impose limits on ideology. In other words, the speaker of Newspeak focuses the destructive power of ideology on one or other member of the collectivity, and thus himself gains power. At the same time he acquires a sort of charisma, by succeeding in narrowing down – and directing at another – the universal threat of ideology. Stalin knew just how to exploit this ambivalence: no one knew better how to transform the all-pervasive menace of ideology into an apparently circumscribed terror. Paradoxically this was why he achieved absolute power, and why his death caused panic among a great many Soviet citizens. For everybody was terrified to find himself alone in face of ideology, deprived of the mediator who knew so well how to deflect its thunderbolts. Confronted by the terror of nothingness which ideology brings, man instinctively seeks refuge under the wing of some tyrant, unaware that in so doing he is handing himself over to the very thing he fears. Compared with sheer nothingness, tyranny always looks like the lesser evil.

But Newspeak does more than articulate ideology and change it into power: it also regulates the distribution of the power. That is to say imparts authority to the same degree that it emphasizes obedience to ideology. In other words, the subject gains power to the extent that he has also displayed submission.

Newspeak has, then, a double role: on the one hand it refracts and amplifies the power of ideology – so that whoever initiates a 'sovspeech' demonstrates the power ideology has over him, while simultaneously acquiring an authority which threatens the other members of the collectivity. For example, by stating: 'It is necessary to show increased vigilance', the orator testifies simultaneously to his loyalty to the ideological fiction of the 'enemies within' and to his aggressive intentions towards his fellows. *Langue de bois* has therefore this unique quality, without precedent in human communication: it can exhibit at the same time both the humiliation of the individual, his inner abasement, and his willingness to pass on the same degradation to others. If Newspeak cannot be called 'economical' from a linguistic point of view, from the viewpoint of power it is, on the contrary, eminently economical.

Not content with increasing power in geometrical progression, Newspeak spreads power throughout society. Every individual can make a speech in Newspeak and so enjoy his momentary share in power. Moreover – and here the regulatory function of Newspeak becomes clearer – the individual possesses that small share of power only in so far as he can operate faultlessly in Newspeak: in other words to the extent that he can demonstrate his fidelity to ideology. Newspeak makes it possible to recruit without risk of error, the sort of leaders and officials that are necessary to the Communist state.[7] And as soon as one understands the selection process, one can no longer harbour any doubts about the continuity of the governing class in Communist countries. It is yet another of ideology's tricks that it manages to depict the power Stalin wielded as personal power, while in reality he became omnipotent only because of his unusual flair for ideology, and his extraordinary mastery of *langue de bois*.

More important still than to select of the faithful is to pinpoint the potential dissident. Here too Newspeak comes in very handy. Not only in regard to speech but in regard to silence. For in a Communist regime, silence can reveal more than words: to say nothing is to compromise oneself; hence the opposition is crushed before it can put its ideas into words; that is, before it can communicate itself. Thanks to Newspeak, Communist preventative action is almost infallible. The right to express oneself has been given to the people: woe betide anyone who does not use it. Power is total only if everyone participates in it: through Newspeak, each man shows, as we have seen, that he is simultaneously the subject and the object of that power – object in so far as he displays his submission to the Party line, subject because he peremptorily invites others to do likewise.

Stalin, then, accepted language as a medium for three reasons. First, because language forces ideology to transmute itself into power – absolute power for the one with the initiative to originate 'wooden' formulations and make others voice them. Second, language distributes that power throughout society. The Party line, defined from above, is then repeated by the totality of citizens, who in the same movement both avow their loyalty and pass on to others the commands imposed from on high. Lastly, thanks to that language, power always varies in dircct proportion to ideological orthodoxy; while potential dissenters are nullified before they can even give substance to their opposition.

NEWSPEAK AS AN IMAGE OF TERROR

Newspeak does not have just one function – that of linking power and society to ideology. It must give permanent expression to that power; it must show that power is at once arbitrary and limitless and it must also incarnate the violence of power. Newspeak does so in two ways: by flying in the face of all evidence and by not bothering to conceal its own contradictions.

Westerners, in their naivety, are astonished at the enormity and crudeness of Communist lies and at the spectacular U-turns made by leading Communists. Far from being a mark of weakness, these incredible lies and sensational recantations advertize the absolute hold which totalitarian regimes have on their subjects. Let it be said again, it is not a matter of conviction; when the Soviet citizen repeats what he knows to be false and utters slogans which contradict those he uttered a little while before, he is merely showing his continuing readiness to follow the Party line; which is all that is required of him. The greater the lie, the more pronounced the policy reversal, the more resoundingly is power affirmed: its impudent disregard for reality and memory is the measure of the brutality it can use without fear of redress.

In the middle of the shambles which followed collectivisation and at the height of the terror, Stalin uttered the
notorious slogan: 'Life has got better: life has become
happier.' It immediately recalls the motto which Himmler
inscribed on the concentration camps: '*Arbeit macht frei*',
'Work makes man free'. The arrogant and repeated
assertion of power is a permanent function of Newspeak.
But it is in the slogans written across the walls of labour
camps that the contempt and cynicism of Newspeak appear
most clearly. Solzhenitsyn gives several examples in 'The
Gulag Archipelago':

'Solovki[8] for workers and peasants.'

'Give the workers what is due to them.' 'We owe everything
– no one owes us anything.' 'Let a surge of the competitive
spirit give the lie to the new slanders of the capitalists about
forced labour in the U.S.S.R.'

Building-sites on the white sea canal of evil memory were
embellished with the following slogans: 'We will drown the
past deep in the canal.' 'This land of pits and marshes will
become our joyful fatherland.' 'Fighting with shovels, we
have dug up happiness close to Moscow.'[9]

Chinese camps are adorned with similar inscriptions
bordering on black humour. Such examples are: 'Understand what is happening', 'Work with enthusiasm', 'Your
future will be glorious', 'Be grateful to the State', etc.[10]

Obviously these slogans are not intended to persuade the
prisoner how fortunate he is: on the contrary their purpose
is to remind him that there is no remedy for his abasement,
that the regime feels free to treat reality with the same
contempt as it treats him, and that reality, so defied, is, like

himself, without redress. These cheery slogans are inflicted on him in order to sustain his despair, reminding him that the whole universe is party to his degradation and, consequently, that nowhere can he find salvation. From this viewpoint, every citizen victimized by Newspeak is a prisoner. The official statements he must absorb and at times repeat all manifest the same contempt for truth and the same claim to omnipotence. He too is completely demoralized by the contrast between the silence of the evidence and the inexhaustible aplomb of the ideology.

Via Newspeak, therefore, Communist power shows that nothing can prevent its piling up affronts alike to its subjects and to truth. It can calmly assert that slavery is happiness, that famine is abundance, that preparations for war arise from love of peace; and no voice will be heard in protest. And yet it still is not enough to abuse sense and conscience: power becomes truly absolute only when it can compel every individual to speak against himself. Self-criticism is the supreme achievement of all Communist regimes.[11] The characteristic aggressivity of Newspeak never appears more clearly than when it is directed against the person speaking it. In such cases, also, Newspeak is used like a magic spell to ward off evil fate: by voluntarily accusing oneself of all sorts of crimes, one hopes to limit the inevitable punishment. In reality, all one achieves is to reinforce power in two ways: one displays one's abject submission to it and one does so publicly, so that other citizens, not fooled by the performance, can judge the extent of the power which is able to compel men to give evidence against themselves.

Ideology cannot master reality, it can only destroy it. It has then to find other ways of manifesting itself in the real world: hence the triple war which Newspeak wages, against facts, against the past, against men. Thanks to the *langue de bois*, ideological power gains substance even if ideology itself is a nullity. Thanks to it, ideology insinuates itself throughout society: thanks to it, ideology can overcome setbacks which would spell the downfall of any other regime and turn them into instruments of strength.

NEWSPEAK AND CIVIL SOCIETY

The most formidable thing about Soviet Newspeak is the way in which it occupies the terrain exluding everything else. A society never becomes completely subjected to power unless the bonds between individuals and groups are enfeebled and unreliable. Newspeak does much to establish this necessary pre-condition. All of its territory is stolen from ordinary language. Newspeak is a one-way operative: it allows no reply. The only possible response to one wooden discourse is another. One can, in extreme circumstances defend[12] oneself in the language of wood – while still displaying fidelity to the Party line – but in no case can one speak without distorting one's meaning. Communication is thereby short-circuited throughout the whole public sphere in which Newspeak alone reigns. Forming social ties becomes almost impossible because an idiom whose only external referent is force can scarcely foster human solidarity. Newspeak moves from top to bottom – one conveyor-belt among others. For a citizen of a Communist state, all forms of public life are connected with Newspeak: in other words, more or less openly linked to the 'correlations of forces'. Civil society is permanently crippled by its lack of an appropriate language. Ordinary language, which survives (in part at least) in private life, is not strong enough to weave the true fabric of civil society. For instance genuine legal language does not exist, it is spirited away or by-passed by Newspeak. Nor does the abstract vocabulary, for instance of philosophy, which the language of Communism has raped and totally distorted.

From this standpoint, one may say that Newspeak is complementary to economic planning.[13] Deprived of economic initiative, society becomes deprived also of the power of speech. It can move neither into the practical world of economics nor into the symbolic worlds of linguistic creation. Like planning, Newspeak cannot completely deny existence to society. But it can freeze that society and force it to live in slow motion and to vegetate in extremely primitive forms. Each individual starts, as it were, from nothing and has to master language without the benefit of the experience of others and without the power to transmit what he has learned. Each individual attempt remains isolated and society at large remains stagnant, because the movement of ideas, like the movement of goods, is blocked. The work of Alexander Zinoviev gives a clear insight into this social marking time, which he manages to represent in the very literary forms that he employs. He displays the insulation which develops among men when the spoken word is everywhere regarded with suspicion. By arousing mistrust towards language in general Newspeak succeeds in bringing civil society to a halt.

Newspeak is the main instrument of the totalitarian state. Without it, power would be obliged to confine itself to fixed, localized situations; and then that atmosphere of universal menace typical of ideological power would be lost. Without Newspeak, power could wear off as well as its possessors or even fall into wrong hands. Without it, power could not completely infiltrate society; and so ideology would remain a dead letter with no hold on human life. Without Newspeak, society would in the last resort be able to protect itself against the aggression of ideology with a barrier of traditions, relationships and contracts. Communist ideology makes language into an arbitrary phenomenon and thus ends by discrediting language itself, in other words, by cutting man off from humanity.

Notes to Chaper III

[1] Ibid, p. 31

[2] Ibid, p. 34

[3] J. Stalin, *Marxism and the Linguistic Question*, Berlin, 1962, p. 18

[4] For Marr's teaching and the linguistic stances of Stalin, see the work of L.L. Thomas, *The Linguistic Theories of N. Marr*, Berkeley, 1957.

[5] E. Benveniste, 1966, p. 259.

[6] In our interpretation of this minor work of Stalin's, we are much indebted to an article by Alexander Wat, *'Semantyka jezyka stalinskiego'* in *Aneks* 21, 1979. See also L. Rzhevskiy, 1951, pp. 46 on.

[7] In connexion with the wooden language L. Martinez speaks of a 'monstrous Latin of a monstrous Church'. See L. Martinez, 'Langue de bois Soviétique', in *Commentaire*, winter 1982-83, no.16, pp. 506-515.

[8] Translator's note: The Solovki Islands were a prison camp notorious for its harsh conditions and for being virtually escape-proof. The camp was one of the first in the Soviet Union, established in the 'twenties.

[9] In: A. Solzhenitsyn, *Gulag Archipelago*, London 1974.

[10] Quoted in: J. Pasqualini, *Prisoner of Mao*, London, 1975.

[11] This practice has been brought to perfection by the Chinese Communists – some very fine examples of self- criticism are given in J. Pasqualini, op. cit.

[12] Barbusse gives a touching report of a conversation between Stalin and a Party official, which provides a splendid example of the defensive use of Newspeak:

Stalin: How are the sowings in your area?

Official: We have mobilised for them, Comrade Stalin.

Stalin: Good, and now?

Official: There has been a change for the better, Comrade Stalin, we will soon have a change for the better.

Stalin: Good, but what next?

Official: We proceeded to improvement projects.

Stalin: So, then, how are the sowings?

Official: At the moment, Comrade Stalin, no success was achieved.

[13] In this connexion see A. Besançon, *Anatomie d'un spectre*, Calmann-Lévy, 1981

IV

THE NEW MAN

– What does intelligence consist of?

– What does it consist of?   In believing one's eyes and not one's ears.

Solzhenitsyn, *Cancer Ward*

'I didn't speak, I was thinking,' he said. 'As long as one hasn't spoken, one is not intelligent. In silence there is no intelligence – there is only the agony of feeling.'

Platonov, *Chevengur*

The Communist regime has always proclaimed its intention to create a 'new man'. Has he arrived? In other words, has communism managed to change radically the mentality and behaviour of its subjects? It is impossible to give a definitive answer to this crucial question. But one can tackle it via literature, one of the few witnesses we have of the Soviet mental world and of the impact of Newspeak on the thought and psychology of the 'new man'.

THE NEW MAN AT SCHOOL

Newspeak is central to the early training of the 'new man'. From childhood, the Soviet citizen is steeped in it. The teaching in the schools – except, of course, scientific teaching – is actually in Newspeak. Even foreign languages are studied in their 'wooden' version. In French, for example, extracts from *l'Humanité*, even translations of Lenin, are used. A Westerner can hardly imagine how wooden pedagogy closes round each young Soviet citizen. Consider this advice to primary teachers from professional pedagogues:

Images of Soviet-socialist society are formed during the process of teaching the whole curriculum (...) However, each subject has its own objectives and potential. For example, the syllabus for reading aims to induce in children through the use of literature, typical images of the life and toil of Soviet citizens, of V.I. Lenin and the Soviet Communist Party, of the life of the workers before and after the Great Socialist October Revolution, of the building of socialism in the U.S.S.R., of the achievements of the Soviet people since the start of the Soviet regime, of its victory in the Great Patriotic War, of the moral stance of the Soviet citizen, of the friendship and cooperation between Soviet peoples, of the Soviet people's struggle for peace and progress and of Communism (...) Experienced teachers know that the aim of the reading syllabus is not to give children as much factual information as possible but to exercise a positive influence on the formation of their feelings and their intellectual, moral, civic and aesthetic opinions through their comprehension and awareness of the events and phenomena shown in works of fiction (...) The task of developing images of Soviet socialist society is not limited to lessons in reading (...) The natural science syllabus is also an opportunity for showing in detail how the Communist Party and Soviet government have given proof of their care for the people's health, their conditions of work and their leisure (...)

The visual arts and music have great potential for socio-political education (...) The visual arts can give rise to discussions on such themes as 'V.I. Lenin in the work of Soviet artists', 'Fields and workplaces of our country', which help pupils to organise and generalize their knowledge of the great events in the life of the Soviet people, of our guide and of the ardour of work in Socialist and Communist edification (...) The songs about Lenin, the Party, our Fatherland, its heroic exploits and events, the happy lives of Soviet children, who are given music lessons, have also helped to train the emotions. In these ways the subjects studied in the primary schools create conditions favourable to the production of images of the Soviet socialist system in the minds of children[1] (...)

If one remembers that all Soviet teachers are required to follow that advice and have no freedom to vary their teaching, one can get some idea of the education that young Soviet citizens receive. In the same way that the aim of the Soviet Press is to comment in such a way as to do away with reality by overwhelming it, so the effect of wooden pedagogy is to give an education which suppresses culture. But this is not only a matter of starving the mind, because, as Voltaire wrote: 'Even the little that we know extends the power of the soul.'[2] 'Wooden' education forces children to unlearn the ordinary language that they have begun to pick-up from their families. The endless repetition of the dogma and myths of ideology is not intended to strengthen the conviction among pupils that Communism is the highest condition of the human race. In fact, there is much evidence to show that the ideological pounding tends to provoke the opposite reaction; one of derision and rejection. It is well-known that Soviet pupils make up jokes about 'Grandpa Lenin' and that many of the most caustic anecdotes going the round in the Soviet Union emanate from schoolchildren. No, pedagogy has another, less obvious, function, which it fulfils effectively. It destroys language as a symbolic system, by inculcating a form of speech that has no meaning. In place of ordinary language based on how things are, it puts a sequence of vocables to summon up what should be. This early side-tracking of ordinary language, together with the absolute monopoly that Newspeak has in the abstract field of the mind, has very serious consequences.

THE DESTABILISATION OF THE SELF

'I' is excluded from language

In a language which is undermined by the need for constant invocation and which has endlessly to proclaim universal dynamism, representation is unachievable, especially the representation of the Self. However:

> It is in and by language that man becomes a subject; because only language establishes the ego in reality; in that reality which is the reality of being. The 'subjectivity' which is discussed here is the ability of a speaker to think of himself as 'subject'. This subjectivity can be defined ... as the psychic unity which transcends all the life-experiences which it comprises and guarantees the permanence of consciousness.
>
> My thesis is that this subjectivity ... is no more than the emergence in being of a basic characteristic of language. 'I' exists because I use 'I' .... Language is only possible because each speaker assumes the role of subject .... The separateness of persons is the fundamental condition of language.[3]

The space which Newspeak occupies while replacing the opposition of 'I' and 'you' by that of 'we' and 'them' is a territory from which the subject, the first person, is banished. The moment 'Soviet man' leaves the world of the tangible where ordinary language reigns, he has great difficulty is perceiving himself as a 'subject'.

The humiliation of the memory

Newspeak hinders the establishing of 'I' in yet another way – it puts a ban on memory. Woe betide anyone who draws attention to the variations and contradictions of the Party line! If he wants a quiet life, he must learn to forget them. Wooden language prevents the true formation of an historical and individual consciousness by making memory dangerous and painful. Memory becomes dangerous because each slogan has to be seen not as ephemeral but as definitive; from that of today back to the very first in 1917. So anything that casts doubt on the order of the day is seen as a dissident act. Memory becomes painful because every single man has, in his public life, committed some cowardly or mean act through the use of Newspeak; and so memory can lead to self-disgust.[4]

Perpetual purposiveness

Once the past has been hidden the present has to be dealt with. Nothing is easier in a country where shortages are chronic. Here, the imperative aspect of Newspeak makes strange contact with the daily reality of Soviet life. There are the thousand things which the Soviet citizen has to do to get enough food and other basic necessities. This predicament coincides in a way with the unending official propaganda calling for greater efforts. Out of necessity, the Soviet citizen is obliged to live in the immediate future and to pursue concrete aims just as ideology would have him do. To obtain the smallest thing requires effort and thought. Scarcely has the citizen satisfied one need than he discovers another even more urgent one.

Propaganda gives each Soviet citizen a place in the headlong development of the Socialist economy, by putting bcfore him a series of new targets which the Plan requires him to meet. In reality, in his daily life, the citizen is inescapably bound up with all sorts of undertakings connected with daily needs. Ideology and real life meet in an unusual and dangerous way: both work in conjunction to annihilate the present and submerge the citizen in a frenzy of activity which allows him no rest; both agree to hand over the present as prey to the future.

The citizen of a totalitarian state is deprived of all those opportunities of personal withdrawal which are necessary to the constitution of a conscious self. He cannot conceive of himself as a separate 'I' resting on the fixed universe of abstract concepts. For these concepts are already raped or destroyed by Newspeak. Memory is either forbidden or made so thoroughly painful that 'Soviet man' can seldom reach psychological or intellectual maturity. He is indeed hard put to it to think of himself as a distinct person.

In general, time for him means exhaustion rather than achievement. Often he seems obsessed with eternity: by its unceasing claim to be definitive, Newspeak creates despair, which is probably the main cause of the citizen's apathy. The present can offer thin compensation, since it is lived in the imperative mood. Thus it always becomes tinged with the stress that is inseparable from being mobilized towards a goal.

SIGNS AND MEANING

The need for 'placing'

One specific characteristic of the psychology of the 'new man' appears clearly in recent Soviet writings, especially in the works of Alexander Zinoviev. Since the feeling of identity among Soviet citizens is not fixed in language or meaning, it tends to be located in a series of exterior signs marking social position. The only principle of personality-coherence is one's position in the social hierarchy; and whatever indicates that position in the eyes of others. Hence the mania for decorations and privileges, great or small, which is typical of Communist states. I. Zemtsov aptly expresses the point:

> Alienation in the USSR goes so deep that if a man is deprived of the external attributes of his existence, his job or his social position, his personality falls apart completely (...). By conferring symbols on a man, the state imposes on him a moral for his own behaviour and for how he should be perceived by others (...). Besides, this depersonalising process is so far gone and takes such a hold on a man that, without realizing it, he comes to need unceasingly all those external factors which establish his existence.[5]

For that reason, the life of Soviet emigrés is often a tragedy. The whole system of distinctions which enables them to 'place' themselves, even negatively, *at home* has been brutally removed and the fragility of the ego is now felt as a kind of suffering.[6]

One can reasonably argue that the fondness for medals and decorations, the tendency to value oneself exclusively by one's social position, and the frenzy to be part of the hierarchy are nothing new in Russia. One has only to read Gogol or Chekhov to know that is the case. The old system of official ranking favoured that sort of psychology. But the Soviet regime has greatly extended these inclinations.

The durability of wooden categories.

How Newspeak works is shown by the unprecedented fact that thoughts and words are equally subordinate to this popular wish for social status. Thus people display marks or signs which prove that they belong to the camp of the Good. Soviet citizens tend to underestimate the role of Newspeak, since they do not see the profound corruption that it brings to thought. They are not aware that the illusion that one is thinking fluently (an illusion induced by the abundance of ready-made formulae) persists even after one has ceased to believe the ideology. Moreover, anyone who succeeds in exposing the ideology's lies thinks he has accomplished a tremendous intellectual feat which absolves him from further effort. In reality, he has fulfilled only a pre-condition of mental maturity. In most cases he stops there unaware that to free oneself intellectually one has to do more than dissipate the ruling fictions. One must also rid oneself of all the mannerisms of wooden thought, that is, one must stop making value-judgements as a substitute for searching for meaning. One must find meaning again.

Moreover if one scrutinises dissidents' writings from this viewpoint, one sees how few of them actually escape from manicheism: most think it sufficient to reverse the values given to words by Newspeak, so that words with a positive significance in Marxist-Leninist ideology acquire a negative one and vice versa – whence the denunciations of material-ism, the exaltation of spirituality and of the nation as a mystical body, etc. By way of example, I here present an analysis of an article which appeared in *Kontinent*[7] from the pen of a certain Victor Trostnikov, which contains the principal themes of a number of dissident writings.

The author begins with a condemnation of the 20th century: 'Our century, deprived of spirituality, is materialis-tic (...). The absence of spirituality gives rise to a materialism which is both philosophical and existential (...). Philosophy, by definition, is the science of the hidden essence of things, the search for the real meaning behind appearances. For the materialist, things are an end in themselves: behind the surface of phenomena he feels no depth, no mystery.'

There follows a condemnation of societies based on a materialist philosophy, then a condemnation of 'hedonistic' societies, that is, those which practice existential material-ism. The author blames them in these words: 'Little by little, the centre of gravity moves towards the more primitive aspects of man, to biology and eventually to physiology. This process of reduction develops steadily, because for the man deprived of spirituality the lowest feelings and crudest instincts are more simple, more certain and more real than refined emotions. The result is that, over eighty years, hedonistic societies have changed greatly, and for the worse.' Their error is to take account of only a limited aspect of man whereas 'only infinity possesses unlimited scope and therefore the meaning of life can be conceived and felt only in infinite categories.' The conclu-sion is simple. 'The Russians must be cured of their totalitarianism, the Americans and West Europeans, of their democracy.'

The author continues with an eloquent diatribe against 'the fetish of democracy': 'A few moments' thought will suffice to show one that no truth can be arrived at by adding up votes (...). "The people" is not the sum of individuals, but a sort of mystical super-organism, which has its own means of expressing itself.' Democracy is dangerous 'because it ends history and takes away the object of man's collective life'. Science also no longer finds favour with our author: 'for a long time now (...) men of science have been bogged down in lies.' As for politicians, they are just as contemptible because they 'firmly believe in the possibility of constructing paradise by man's hands'. They understand nothing because 'their thoughts are fragmentary'. The article ends on this bombastic note:

> Such is the trivial outcome of the great revolution which began in the age of humanism or Renaissance. Men took against God, because He had not freed them from suffering; and they decided to use their own means to make a life without suffering. The result of man's abandoning God was that the mystical roots which nourished nations with their life-giving sap were destroyed and people who had been united saw themselves transformed into collections of separate citizens (...)

What strikes one first here is the presence of the customary axiological matrix, but with certain values inverted. Materialism has become a negative pole, spirituality a positive one. Science is in the camp of Evil, as is 'humanism', both formerly very much approved of by the official ideology. Society remains the arena of an irreversible process. However, this time the process is degrading and not a means of progress. One notices that the scheme of Newspeak is presented quite intact: the opposition of appearance and reality, the claim to be all-embracing, the

denunciation of 'the fetish of democracy' – Lenin's phrase –
in the 'fragmentary thinking', the idea that history has a
pre-ordained end, and idea of the collective as superior to
the separate individual. The author has not managed to
break out of the circuit within which thought is held captive
by Newspeak.

Soviet teaching simply does not allow any other sort of
thinking. It especially excludes all thought which could
properly be called political: political thought is far from
easy. The book which Igor Chafarevich[8] devoted to
socialism is another example of the powerful magnetism of
the 'wooden' categories. Chafarevich demonstrates that
socialism has always existed, either as theory or in political
form. For him, socialism is the embodiment of a society's
death-wish. It is interesting to see how, at the end of his
book, the author regrets that he seems to have arrived at a
sort of dualism. 'It would be distressing if the ideas I have
expressed represented in the last analysis a sort of dualism,
because that is an unstable and fragmented view of the
world (...).'[9] In fact, the unwanted dualism forced on
Chafarevich is the price of omitting the historical dimension, rather like the sociology of Zinoviev. All this shows to
what extent the categories of the *langue de bois* take over
from those of ideological thought. Newspeak banishes time,
while ideology tries to be historical. Neither Chafaverich
nor Zinoviev turns away from the historical point of view
because they find it corrupted by ideology: they simply do
not possess this viewpoint, having grown up under the sign
of the eternal and the definitive.

Discourse about virtue

The difficulty which dissidents find in gaining access to
genuine thought derives not only from the need to give up

the mental comfort of generalizations, of broad unclear
models and binding affirmations disguised as logical deduc-
tions. In a word, it is not only a question of overcoming the
temptation of easy thinking. There is more to the switch-
over than that. One has also to come to terms with the
objective i.e. neutral meanings of words; and to do that it is
essential to stop seeing language as a network of social
indicators guaranteeing the coherence of Self. Within the
Soviet system, using Newspeak amounts to an act of loyalty
to the system. For many dissidents the language remains a
way of giving signals rather than expressing thought – a way
of showing that the speaker's position is one of siding with
the Good. In other words, the language remains a sign of
loyalty, only the nature of the Good changes – whence
those discourses on Virtue which are sometimes so irritating
in the writings of emigrés typified by the works of Maximov.
Here is an example taken from *The Saga of the Rhinoceros*.
The narrator is speaking to a journalist, a ' modern pagan
with plenty in the bank' and reports the latter's words:

> You Russians are odd people. You are prepared to go on
> endlessly discussing questions which the civilized world
> resolved ages ago and are no longer on its agenda (...).

The narrator reacts sharply:

> (...) And what is your background, you who are neat and
> spruce and have already settled all life's problems and
> removed God Himself from the agenda? He really is most
> merciful to tolerate people like you blaspheming against His
> name and to forgive you all your luxuries. His patience is
> inexhaustible, but can ordinary men be so tolerant? When
> they see and hear political nonentities, who are motivated
> by greed and the desire for power, trying to win over the
> crowd by the bogus prospectus of a new share-out – a
> share-out from which they will anyhow get nothing – will

they be able to resist? And as for you, millions of victims
shot, burnt, tortured to death, starved in the name of
'goodwill to all men', from Prague to Kolyma, come and
testify! (....) No Huns, no Inquisition could have invented all
that – an evil never seen anywhere in the world even in the
darkest ages![10]

Newspeak appears in every line of this text, in its pathos,
in the extreme aggressivity of tone, in the allegorical
depiction of the enemy, that same smug bourgeois who
provokes the thunderbolts of the Soviet press. Just as in
Newspeak the revelation of truth is accompanied by an
outburst of emotion which suspends judgement, so that
agreement seems obligatory.

This 'discourse of Virtue' is not the same thing as jargon,
since it is not intended to convey membership of a particular
social category. Its vocabulary is not, for example, like
those slang terms which signify membership of a group,
while having no existential implications. On the contrary
the vocabulary indicates a 'will-to-be' and a 'will-to-do' and
shows the author's wish to be identified with an 'us' that
carries every positive overtone.

Ideological manicheism continues to offer its frame of
reference to individuals, who speak to affirm their position
and not to express a point of view. By heaping up
invocations to Virtue, the Soviet citizen holds up before
himself the imperatives which conjure away the ever-
present threat: the disintegration of his personality. For him
the moral content is not the expression of a re-discovered
freedom; it is, rather, a revelation of the precariousness of a
Self which can realize itself only as the object of imperatives
because it is deprived of duration and representation. Not
surprisingly moral preaching takes a growing place in
official Soviet publications under Gorbachev's *glasnost*.
Never have 'truth', 'good', 'courage', 'freedom' been
mentioned so often. The traditional ideological lexicon is

partly sacrificed, but the underlying ideological framework is thus preserved: Gorbachev's words are labels signalling one's allegiance to the camp of the good, that is, of *perestroika* – in other words, of the present Party line.

The new man: language and consciousness

If one takes 'the new man' to mean the fanatical robot portrayed by Zamiatin in his book *We*, one can say that wooden education has ended in failure. Soviet man is not an unfeeling cog in an inhuman machine. His bombardment by propaganda leads him to indifference or irony. But one may wonder, especially after reading the novels of Zinoviev, whether developed socialism really has any need of fanatics. According to Zinoviev and Neizvestny, socialism depends most of all on the manoeuvrings of careerists; and from this viewpoint, Newspeak is completely successful. A go-getter without any talent will find ideology to be an ideal means to promotion. So a typically Soviet form of ambition develops, which Zinoviev has so well described: no will to accomplish anything at all, not even to achieve real power, but instead a perpetual thirst for the exterior signs of social success, a constant dissatisfaction fuelled by envy, by a genius for bluffing and by a mindless hatred of real talent.

The dissolution of identity by Newspeak shows itself sociologically in the ubiquitous careerism which finds so many opportunities in Soviet society. The U.S.S.R., with its innumerable hierarchical distinctions, is a careerist's paradise. Is this destabilization felt by the Soviet individual at all? Is his consciousness different from one entirely structured by ordinary language? Once again, literature can give us some clues.

The 'lyrical consciousness'

One thing is certain: all-pervading Newspeak in the end provokes a distrust of language in general. Every statement becomes suspect: truth deserts the word. This instinctive rejection of the deceitful word is the origin of what one might call 'lyrical consciousness'. The search for a reality beyond words involves an act of empathy towards things, especially towards nature. Often it takes the form of a longing for friendly speechless human contacts. All the works of Andrei Platonov, a writer of the nineteen-twenties, are really an exploration of the lyrical consciousness. His books poignantly reveal the anguish of a man always open to the world and spontaneously reaching out to others, who is yet prevented by his total openness from perceiving himself.

> The eternal essence which has no need to move, nor to live, nor to die, replaced in him something forgotten, but necessary, like the presence of a lost friend.[11]

> Sometimes he loved to remain in silence, watching all that passed into his view. Thinking was difficult and that saddened him. He was forced to hold on to his feelings and emotions without being able to put them into words.[12]

Here Platonov described the effect produced on a crowd by a speech given by a trade union offical – in *langue de bois*, of course:

> (...) Some listened to him in order to fill the anguished vacuum in their minds with his words; others gave themselves up to their own uniform sadness, preferring to live inside their own silence, without hearing anything he said.[13]

Typical is Platonov's analysis of the state of mind of soldiers enlisted in the Red Army during the Civil War:

They did not yet know those things in life which are precious (...). That is why there were no chains in their souls to fix their attention onto themselves. That is why they lived a full life in communion with nature and history, and history at that time was steaming ahead like an express train (...).[14]

Chepurny absorbed life piece by piece. Fragments of a world he had known long before and memories of encounters floated in his head as in a still lake; but these fragments never came together, and for Chepurny they had no link and made no living sense (...). He knew every word of Lenin's teachings, but all these clear memories floated at random in his mind without forcing anything meaningful.[15]

Kopionkin knew nothing in particular, because he lived his life without trying to preserve it through a vigilant consciousness endowed with the gift of memory.[16]

A feeling could last for a long time within Kopionkin – even years. He could only lead his internal life in despair: a despair moderated by the performance of just deeds.[17]

Perhaps only the artist's insight could reveal the consequences of this turning away from the mediation of language that Marr wished for. The poetic writings of Platonov contain a true diagnosis of this new aphasia, which is doubtless a distinctive feature of the 'new man'. No one has ever understood better than Platonov the tragedy of the 'lyrical consciousness'. When a man's stubborn sense of reality is threatened by ideology there results a state of alienation which is like suffering. Thought becomes painful and almost impossible. Memory itself becomes destructive and helps to dissolve the personality instead of strengthening it. Feelings and impressions fight over a consciousness that is open to everything and unable to find shelter in concepts. Deprived of abstract thought, man exhausts himself in a bottomless anxiety.

Platonov understood that, in such a state, any form of words becomes welcome; thus ideological discourse finds its way easily into lyrical consciousness.

In the town of Chevengur, where Communism has been established, a Bolshevik, Prokofy, has the task of formulating all statements. He is the only unsympathetic character in the novel, because he lives a self-centred life while the others exhibit complete altruism. But, in spite of Prokofy's obvious petit-bourgeois tendencies, they cannot manage without him. At one moment, Chepurny, the main proponent of Communism in Cherengur, addresses him in these words:

> – Formulate, Prochka, I feel something.[18]

So the circle closes: by allowing their disbelief in Newspeak to contaminate their faith in ordinary language, Platonov's heroes condemn themselves to a painful absence of the Self which impels them to enter wholeheartedly into the vice-like grip of ideological language and into wild adventures where action itself momentarily produces a semblance of being. Soon, however, the well-founded distrust of organised expressions of thought returns; and once more reality rushes in and the Self crumbles away.

Platonov shows admirably that the feeling for reality, however strong it is (or, rather, especially if it is strong) is of no help against the magnetism of ideology. Necessarily the sense of reality cannot give access to the truth unless it has a language through which it can implant itself in consciousness without overwhelming it.

Platonov is not the only Soviet writer to reveal this instinct for the lyrical consciousness. One can discover it in

a number of authors, Pasternak for example, who cele-
brates a mystique of life and the union with nature. Nor is
the lyrical consciousness expressed only in literature.
Everyone who has lived in the Soviet Union has noticed
how nature acts as a release, how people seek oblivion in it
and purification, and how they experience a metamorphosis
through contact with nature. The individual gives himself
up completely to communion with nature in a Rousseau-
es,que ecstasy, which is all the more powerful because it is
an escape from a truly perverse civilization.

Another outward sign of the lyrical consciousness is the
Russian inclination towards alcoholism. Nothing is better
than vodka at making close contact between men and men
and men and things. Vodka dissolves lies and eventually
makes language useless. Like nature, it produces a feeling
of existence which by-passes awareness of Self. The
dumbness of those drunkards who inhabit real socialism
corresponds to that of Platonov's heroes working to build
the communist Utopia. But drunkenness is not only the
lyrical consciousness, which of course belongs to the first
stage of intoxication. Other mental states follow that are
equally characteristic of 'Soviet man'. Venedict Erofeev's
book *Moscow-on-the-Vodka* contains a long monologue by
a drunkard. The work describes with astonishing mastery
the various mental states of the 'new man': alcohol does not
create them, it simply speeds up their procession through
his being.

The 'viscous consciousness'

The instability of the Self in the Soviet world is revealed
though lyrical consciousness. Another effect of Newspeak –
the absence of representation – is what the sculptor Ernst
Neizvestny calls 'the viscous consciousness'. Instead of

handling concepts, the mind is put into motion entirely by verbal associations. It is carried along by the torrent of words it produces. There again, the speaker himself is not present in this discourse of his, which is fashioned, as it were automatically, into a string of phrases and slogans. As there is no thought, a cataract of insignificant details drown any meaning the whole might have. The words latch onto anything and nothing. Here is Neizvestny's description in which the 'viscous consciousness' is represented by an important Party dignitary:

> He was noted for his viscous consciousness and for getting entangled in meaningless detail which in the end bogged him down. The external world of objects detracted him from his theme (...). Here are some samples of his conversation:
> My wife [here we are given her curriculum vitae: origins, age, police record, education, plus height, colour of hair and eyes and other physical characteristics] did not believe I would succeed in life (...). But it is sometimes nice to show people where they get off. One day someone telephoned me ... [now we get the story of his telephone being installed, with generalizations about the usual installation of telephones and details of *his* telephone, designed to show how superior it is to other people's.] I am summoned to a meeting .... At whose house do you think? Molotov's! (...). My wife is watching me, with a puzzled expression, from behind the curtains ... [Information about his curtains and curtains in general.] (...)[19]

The viscous consciousness latches on, even more willingly, to details, because they are also a sort of signal: once again, meaning takes second place to social indicators. On other occasions, the viscous consciousness is beguiled not by external things but by the force of language itself. Then, as with *langue de bois*, purely linguistic mechanisms operate to produce speech: one word gives rise to another; one saying leads to another; the author is caught up in the auto-mechanisms of language. There are some very good examples of these drifts of verbal diarrhoea in *Moscow-on-the-Vodka*. A dissertation on hiccups opens with the following weighty considerations:

> To begin this study it is obviously necessary to induce a hiccup: either *an sich* – Immanuel Kant's phrase – that is to say, to introduce it for its own sake, or to make it happen in another person, but in his own interest, that is to say, *für sich*. Again, the term is Kant's. Obviously the best solution is *an sich* and *für sich*, and this is the way to tackle it: for two hours on end drink something strong (...).[20]

A few pages further on, the narrator meditates on territorial frontiers:

> Our border-guards know perfectly well that the frontier is neither fiction nor a symbol, because on one side of the frontier people speak Russian and drink a lot, while on the other side they drink less and do not speak Russian .... But beyond that? How could there be frontiers if everybody drank to the same extent and did not speak Russian? (...). So much so that it could lead from this point of view to full freedom. For example – you wish to stop at Eboli: all right, stop at Eboli. You wish to go to Canossa: no one is stopping you, go to Canossa. You wish to cross the Rubicon: cross it.[21]

As well as illustrating the automatic linkages between words, this passage shows another feature of Newspeak: the false logical progression that is a counterfeit of true reasoning. The string of phrases hides the paralysis of thought and the passivity of the speaker himself during his speech.

Attachment to the surface of words and things is frequent

in Soviet writings, even for those uninfluenced by alcohol. It arises from the unavailability of abstract thought and from a simultaneous movement of defence and rejection. Only completely trivial utterances can be neutral, in the sense that they compromise neither the speaker nor the ideology. So the subject deliberately sets out to be absent from what he expresses: empty words are a necessary condition for survival, or at least for social promotion. Everything, then, leads the New Man towards the viscous consciousness. From childhood, he had used a language detached from meaning and now he must reveal nothing of himself to the unfriendly scrutiny of others. Thus the flow of futile words that emanates from the viscous consciousness seems to be an inevitable complement to ideological speech.

The 'parodical consciousness'

In the case of the viscous consciousness, the speaker is unaware of his subjection to language, because his mind follows the path of the words he has used. However, when he is more intelligent, he perceives this alienation in and through language. He realizes that the language he uses is often inadequate; and he will then resent the obligation to talk Newspeak as something demeaning. The less he is subject to ideological terms, the less the individual can find in himself excuses to justify his compromises with Newspeak. As long as he has to protect his very life by demonstrating his loyalty, the situation is psychologically bearable. But when he has to produce speech which he well knows to be inept, merely in the hope of getting social promotion by eliminating a competitor, the poor fellow becomes prey to self-disgust and self-loathing.

Thus there arises what one might call the 'parodical

consciousness,' of which there are many examples in Soviet literature. This type of consciousness is also the basis of Soviet humour. Alexander Zinoviev is its great literary representative; and it his work that best displays the origin and implications of this parodying mode of discourse. It explains the vicious circle which imprisons the individual in the countries of real socialism. In this situation the subject can organise himself only through purposiveness, which takes the form of a striving for power and social advancement. But such a career is possible only if the subject is ready to talk Newspeak when the occasion demands. The subject feels his alienation from real life as a humiliation with two consequences: first, he flees from himself; that is to say, he cannot reconstitute natural language because in doing so he would make his suffering real. Second, he looks everywhere around him for replications of his own degradation. For only a full-dress collective self-abasement could help to rehabilitate him in his own eyes. But then the abasement of the others confirms his disgust for life and for himself. So Newspeak not only destroys the personality of the subject, it also obliterates his ego and, as it were, drives him out of himself. Worse still, the world around him seems so awful as to be unworthy of description. As Zinoviev says so forcefully in *Yawning Heights*:

> The world we experience does not lend itself to verbal description. Everything is either formless to the point of invisibility or nauseatingly clear-cut and angular. The few things one holds on to for their apparent solidity and importance turn out to be quite trivial or are something that doesn't even have a name. And the boundless morass of words refers to absolutely nothing that is real.[22]

We are faced here with a new type of mutism just as formidable as the lyrical consciousness overwhelmed by material things, or the pathological logorrhoea of the viscous consciousness. It is a resigned mutism, a voluntary abandonment of language since words can only register the existential distress. Not merely are words deprived of meaning, but the meaning one can assign to them is not worth the trouble.

It will be objected that the 'parodical consciousness' is not in the least dumb, and that one had only to recall Zinoviev's characters to see that. However his writings only make sense insofar as they implicitly make permanent reference to Newspeak; and Zinoviev's grotesque imitation of it does not free him or anyone else from the original. In his words Zinoviev does no more than revive that humiliating moment the speaker and his listeners experienced, when they were the vehicles of Newspeak. The parodical consciousness is basically as malicious as normal Newspeak is essentially aggressive. Both are alike in being self-contained captive languages reflecting isolated souls in a desolate world. The desert which Newspeak brings about, the total famine of intelligence and the suffocation of the spirit, appear at their crudest in the satiric version of Newspeak where derision serves only to demonstrate the general humiliation. Parodic Newspeak certainly allows intelligence to take its revenge, by forcefully revealing the absurdity of ideological discourse; but even this revenge is accompanied by a sense of complicity in man's degradation.

The general debasement is often portrayed by recourse to scatological or trivial themes. Time and time again, ideological speech is ridiculed by the grossest physiological references. For example, in *Moscow-on-the-Vodka* discussions of hiccups cast slurs on the prestige of Marx and Engels. What follows is about hiccup-frequency:

It is said that those guides of the world proletariat, Karl Marx and Friedrich Engels, made a detailed study of patterns of social groupings and that consequently they were able to foresee many things. But in this matter they could foresee nothing at all. With hiccups you enter on your very own into the province of fate – be patient and wait. Life will make a nonsense of your elementary and your advanced mathematics alike (...).[23]

In Zinoviev's writings a director 'dies from diarrhoea of the brain'.[24] Another dignitary poisons the atmosphere in the country with his farts: he has stuffed himself with food from the special shops.[25] But scatological themes are used only incidentally to ridicule dogma and here one can scarcely compare Zinoviev with Rabelais. For Rabelais, coarseness simply reflected his interest in life in all its forms. For Zinoviev, it symbolizes the common degradation of man and the world and the disgust that arises from the spectacle of degradation. This is true also of Erofeev, who skilfully analysed how collective degradation works. In a significant episode[26] the narrator narrowly escapes being given a beating by his drinking companions because he doesn't announce the nature of his needs when he goes to the lavatory: the others deduce from the omission that he despises them.

For Zinoviev, the whole post-Stalin era is placed under the sign of shit:

The more human of them [i.e. the leading comrades] have recently invented a completely new path, watered with urine, surfaced with shit and spattered with snot and saliva.[27]

And this ridiculous fermentation of (....) shit is lived subjectively as if it were a struggle for ideals.[28]

This eruption of scatology and obscenity is not the work of a few particular authors. It is the result of a widespread perception of the reality of Soviet socialism. Hence the astonishing frequency of what the Russians call '*mat*', the collection of extremely gross swearwords which are invading the language. Ernst Neizvestny has put it exactly:

> Today literary Russian is a foreign language. Normal language has become a mixture of convicts' slang and official cliché.

Newspeak now finds itself in a strange union with obscene slang. So the soiling of individual consciousness is registered in speech by scatology and pornography, so that we witness the birth of a monstrous hybrid bred from the cross-fertilization of Newspeak and obscenity. This hybrid is becoming the typical speech of the New Man. It would be wrong to think that this injection of '*mat*' is a threat to Newspeak. For Newspeak is built up in the same way as the swearing-system; it copies its technique of free association of words and stock phrases. Besides one even speaks of '*mat* with many storeys'. This slang co-exists perfectly well with communist language. It simply shows in a different way the brutality which goes with it and of which the speaker is both creator and victim.

The parodical consciousness is in some ways the very opposite of the lyrical consciousness. For it is entirely shut in on itself; the external world cannot help it for the reason that this language has almost ceased to recognize the world. All it takes from nature is physiology, from which in turn it extracts only the grotesque, image of the stupidity of ideology, and of its own vileness. Everything that reaches this type of consciousness throws it back on itself. While the lyrical consciousness is too open to elements from outside, the parodic consciousness cannot escape itself. That does not mean, however, that the subject becomes more stable. On the contrary, he finds it very hard to centre himself on projects which he perceives to be vain or dishonourable but which he has to stick to because he knows no other principle of personal coherence. The chief character of Zinoviev's *The Radiant Future*, torn between his desire to become a corresponding member of the Academy and his awareness that his work is just a load of rubbish, is typical of this quandary. Without his ambition, his personality would fall apart and he would look like a brother to the drunkard in *Moscow-on-the-Vodka*, who talks to the angels. Erofeev's hero has attained the highest peak of parodical consciousness. He docs not hesitate to work out the most ridiculous projects such as making a graph of the drinking bouts of his subordinates. But this last stage of dissolution leads straight to the disintegration of the subject. *Moscow-on-the-Vodka* ends with these words:

Since then I have not recovered my wits and I never shall.[29]

It is hard to doubt the existence of the various features of the Soviet mind catalogued here. But one can always question the role of Newspeak in their development by arguing that they existed long before the revolution. One may rightly remark that Gogol is full of examples of viscous and parodical consciousness; and that in his works, as in those of Dostoyevsky, Chekhov and many others there are many examples of the Russian madness provoked by obsessive ambition. All that is true.

One can simply conclude that the problem of identity has provided many themes in Russian literature. These themes, especially that of the 'double', of insanity, and of the misery of existence, originate in the Romantic Movement and have had the same prominence – if not the same duration – in Western literature. Soviet literature, however, indirectly but uniquely, demonstrates the disintegration of the Self by reproducing the mutilated language of its pathetic heroes: people uncertain of their being and groping for words, ideas and memories. Among Soviet writers the fragility of the 'I' is not a literary theme, it is an element of Soviet reality that literature has to rediscover and to formulate. As soon, that is, as it rejects the official rules. The Soviet writer is at one with his character in trying to recover the natural language. Where Newspeak has a monopoly true literature can have only one aim, which is the recuperation of meaning. Literature becomes the attempt to formulate; a continuous struggle against the unsaid which threatens to swallow up the individual and remain unsayable forever. Thanks to Newspeak, literature eventually inherits this vital role which the Romantics dreamed for it. It becomes the only safeguard against Newspeak, that formidable war-machine which attacks every individual.

The struggle is hard and the stakes are high. For *langue de bois* is both a treatment and a prophylactic. It is prophylactic because it prevents the subject from originating speech, destroys sense and reference and discredits memory. It is a treatment when it makes the Self detestable, other human beings despicable and the world a desert where the Beautiful and the Good are made to share in the same shipwreck. The study of *homo sovieticus* reveals all the implications of the symbolic function in human life. As soon as symbols cease to work properly, there is no longer a nature *joie-de-vivre*. Man then finds himself in the Soviet universe: a world without meaning, without events and without humanity. The New Man is the desperate citizen of this universe.

Notes to Chapter IV

[1] Quoted from: A.M. Pridanceva, *Mladshim skolnikam o konstitutsii S.S.S.R.* Moscow, 1980, p.9 et seq.

[2] Letter to the Abbé Dubos, 30 October, 1738.

[3] Benveniste, 1966, pp. 259-260.

[4] Jean Pasqualini gives a striking example of this sort of instant forgetfulness following on periods of possession by Newspeak. He describes a session of collective hate organised against him by his fellow prisoners. Each of them dutifully expressed his rage towards him, Pasqualini, but when they returned to their cell each of them greeted him warmly, as if nothing whatever had happened: all had been forgotten.

[5] See I. Zemtsov, 'The U.S.S.R. the ruling elite', in: *Grani* no. 109, 1978, p304.

[6] The poet Edward Limonov graphically describes the dramatic breakdown of personality in the absence of familiar distinguishing landmarks. See Edward Limonov, *Le poète russe préfère les grands nègres*, Paris, 1980.

[7] Victor Trostnikov, 'Konets epochi samougozhdeniya' in *Kontinent*, no. 25, 1980, pp. 255-284.

[8] I. Chafarevich, *Le Phénomène socialiste*, Paris, 1977

[9] Ibid, p.337.

[10] N. Maximov, *The Saga of the Rhinoceros*, Frankfurt-am-Main, 1981, pp. 48-49.

[11] Andrei Platonov, *La Fouille*, Lausanne, 1974, p.37.

[12] Ibid, p.45.

[13] Ibid, p.61.

[14] Andrei Platonov, 'The Hidden Man', in: *Time's Passing*, Moscow, 1971, p.143.

[15] Andrei Platonov, *Chevengur*, Paris, 1972, p.157.

[16] Ibid, p.260.

[17] Ibid, p.277.

[18] Ibid, p.199.

[19] Ernst Neizvestny '*Lik-Litso-Lichina*', in *Kontinent*, no. 27, 1981.

[20] Venedict Erofeev, *Moskva-Petushki*, Paris, 1977, p.29.
[21] Ibid, p.48.
[22] A. Zinoviev, *Yawning Heights*, Lausanne, 1976, p.231.
[23] V. Erofeev, 1977, p.30.
[24] A. Zinoviev, 1976, p.123.
[25] Ibid, p.206.
[26] V. Erofeev, 1977, p.14.
[27] A. Zinoviev, 1976, p.134.
[28] Ibid, p.173.
[29] V Erofeev, 1977. p.78.

V

THE HISTORY OF NEWSPEAK

Because of the disturbances, many troubles beset cities, troubles which happen, and always will happen, while human nature remains the same (...). Even the usual sense of words was changed in relation to deeds.

Thucydides, The Peloponesian War, III, 82.

'What about truth? Does the working class have a right to the truth?' asked Voschev.

'The working-class has a right to movement,' said the militant.

A. Platonov, The Search

The real enemy of Russia is the government and the Emperor himself, who have let themselves be seduced by modern ideas, and especially by German philosophy, which is Russia's poison.

J. de Maistre, Correspondance diplomatique

Newspeak as we have described it has been imposed from the top on Russia and its satellites by the victorious Bolshevik party. However, before becoming the official language of the Communist state it had already been spontaneously adapted in the eighteen-sixties by many of the Russian intelligentsia, at a time when ordinary language still existed in competition with it. To retrace the steps by which Newspeak was constituted is to try to understand how and why ordinary language both in philosophy and in politics, was destroyed over a long period by ideological discourse. One has also to explain why ordinary language offered so little resistance to Newspeak's corrupting influence. Something, after all, must already have happened to prepare it for its transformation into an ideological idiom: meaning has to be abandoned before Newspeak, with its characteristic confusion between the descriptive and the normative can assert itself. The whole process goes hand in hand with the establishment of ideology among the Russian intelligentsia. In other words the history of Newspeak coincides with the history of ideology. However, since ideology consists essentially in the victory of words over both thought and things it is useful to approach this history from the specifically linguistic viewpoint.

WAS THE LANGUAGE OF THE FRENCH REVOLUTIONARIES NEWSPEAK?

The most obvious feature of Newspeak, it will be remembered, is its deliberate orientation towards polemics. In that respect it is comparable with the language of the orators of the French revolution, which exhibited all the stylistic consequence of an extreme manicheism. It seemed to people at the time that a new language had appeared and a thoroughly corrupted one at that, as is shown by this passage from a speech by the Deputy Petit, after the 9th Thermidor:

> Robespierre indeed spoke of virtue, but, according to him, virtuous men are in a minority on earth (...). Robespierre indeed spoke of liberty and equality but in such a way that everybody was to obey Robespierre so that he would have no equals at all (...). Robespierre indeed spoke of the Republic, but the Republic was Robespierre himself, with Couthon and St Just. He spoke indeed of truth, but hardly ever stopped using lies to destroy it (...). He proclaimed freedom of his opinions, but that freedom was, for him and his kind, the right to pursue his hypocritical and bloody follies. He spoke of justice but, according to his horrendous code, suspicions were proofs, demi-thought was action and misfortune became a crime. Robespierre spoke of reason but he had seen to it that it was forbidden in France, on pain

of death, to join two ideas together (...). He spoke of
honesty while praising thieves and of humanity over the
bloody corpses of those whose throats had been cut by his
agents (...).

Beginning with the word 'revolution', they took away the
true meaning from every word in the French language (...).
After spreading turmoil, uncertainty and ignorance everywhere, they introduced into the language a host of new
words and epithets with which they pointed at will to those
men and those things which were to be hated or loved by the
befuddled people. Let us remember, citizens, those sermons
of mad cannibals which they so often delivered on this
platform (...) those speeches in which (...) they attempted
to induce folly in our minds and crime in our hearts (...). Let
us remember that those speeches were re-read and repeated
in all the associated People's Societies (...). Then we will
have a true idea of the way in which the hellish morality of
Robespierre and his kind was disseminated (...).

The greatest infamies (...) remained unpunished and
legalised; public morality was outraged; revolutionary
crimes were brazenly misrepresented even under the eyes of
those who had been present when they were committed.
Revulsion at crime was declared to be a crime itself; talent
and genius were proscribed by ignorant and stupid mediocri-
ties; the French language was disfigured by new words
invented by murderers to serve as slogans; lies and false
principles were propagated in speeches made in the name of
the government – such were the causes of the 9th Thermidor
....[1]

After that, it would seem just to speak of the French
Revolution's Newspeak. A language corrupted by violence
and lies such as the one Deputy Petit describes deserves
comparison with the ideological language of the Russian
revolutionaries. Here are some extracts from speeches
made by Robespierre, since he is the orator mentioned:

Only the most ignorant or the most profoundly perverted person could, in such circumstances, make the claim not to be an enemy of one's country while cruelly working to demean those who have the conduct of affairs, to hinder their plans, to vilify their conduct (...). I insist that, under such conditions, it is impossible for the Committee to save the common weal. If anyone does not believe me, I would remind him how evil and widespread are the plots to dishonour and dissolve us, and how many foreigners and internal enemies are subsidizing agents to oppose us. I would remind him that the opposition is not dead, that it is plotting in the recesses of its cells, that the serpents in the Marais are not yet crushed (...). I bind myself never to criticize patriots but I cannot include among the patriots those who wear only the mask of patriotism; and I will denounce the conduct of those two or three traitors who are working for discord and dissension.[2]

The glory of the Convention is to display strength of character and to sacrifice base prejudices on the altar of the salutary principles of reason and philosophy: its glory lies in the salvation of our country and in the strengthening of liberty through our supreme example to all the world.[3]

Noble representatives of the people, you have by your constant effort ascended to the top of the rock of liberty. Take care not to weaken, or the rock will fall back on you in a thousand pieces and cast you to the bottom of the foul morass.[4]

We wish to fulfil the vows of Nature, to implement the destiny of mankind, to realize the promises of philosophy and to release Providence from the long reign of tyranny.[5]

The similarity with wooden language is indeed remarkable. The manicheism, always present, implicitly or explicitly, reveals itself stylistically through the all-pervading pathos. There are numerous figures of speech, often quite mixed, like that 'rock of liberty' of which Robespierre spoke, a rock which, when climbed, can suddenly turn into the rock of Sisyphus. These speeches are intended also to identify the enemy, so that the insults of the French revolutionaries are as numerous and picturesque as those of their Soviet successors. Indeed it is exactly these aspects of the Montagnards' speeches – these 'epithets' intended to surrender 'men and things' to the anger of the public – that impelled Deputy Petit to speak of linguistic corruption.

However, the similarity stops there. The language of the French revolutionaries contains no excess of noun phrases, and no lack of shifters. Above all, one does not find in French-revolutionese any confusion between fact and value, or between indicative and imperative. Moreover each speaker has his own style. The language is stretched to the extreme by the polemical fervour which inspires it and is certainly bloated here and there by hyperbole; nevertheless, its actual structure is not essentially affected. This is because French-revolutionese is not the flat expression of an impersonal teleology. The rhetoric has to convince individual people, in order that Virtue may conquer Vice; and this is a struggle whose outcome is still uncertain.

The French revolutionaries did not withdraw history from the sphere of morals – the sphere in which there has to be a subject. Their ambition was not to create a clear slate or *tabula rasa* on which to inscribe a radiant future. It was on the contrary to restore the civic virtues so as to found a republic inspired by the glorious models of Antiquity. Everything in the French revolutionary rhetoric was referred to the past – to Cicero and Plutarch –and not to an obligatory Utopia whose outline was too shadowy for thought. Moreover, the exhortations of the French revolutionaries had more logic in them than those of the Bolsheviks. For the French, liberty, was above all else a matter of personal decision; and it was natural that they should seek to stimulate the will by the use of a genuine rhetoric. For the French the future had value only insofar as it would retain the memory of present achievement, just as the present was straining to match the great moments of the past:

> This will be a magnificent theme for our descendants. It is already a spectacle worthy of the earth and sky. To contemplate the Assembly of the representatives of the French people standing above an inexhaustible volcano of plots, with one hand bringing to the feet of the eternal creator of all things the homage of a great people and with the other hurling thunderbolts at the tyrants who oppose it.[6]

> The people must rally their spirits by remembering Sparta and Athens and swear to die under the ruins of the Republic, if it runs the danger of being destroyed.[7]

History has no immanent laws: one looks to Nature, not because it is the seat of the future development of all mankind, but because conformity to natural principles is the very essence of that virtue whose reign one hopes to inaugurate. There again, it is rather a matter of a restoration, which depends on acts of the human will. It is significant that when Robespierre attempts an 'organic' metaphor, to conjure up 'the pains of giving birth to liberty', he draws this sharp criticism from Camille Desmoulins:

> Some people (...) believe that everything can be justified by the one sentence: 'we know our present condition is not free, but be patient, one day we shall be free.'
> These people seem to think that liberty, like childhood, has to pass through pain and tears to reach maturity. On the contrary, the nature of liberty is such, that in order to enjoy it one has only to desire it (...). Liberty has neither old age, nor youth. It has one age only, that of strength and energy ....[8]

The enemies of the Revolution are not the remnants of a bygone age, engaged in a futile attempt to stop the locomotive of history. They are corrupt beings, guilty of crimes against Human Reason, Nature and Humanity. They are the more dangerous because nobody knows on whose side history will be. In this system of thought, then, punishment and preventive action are more justified than in Leninism. For it is logical enough that a revolution that proclaims its object to be the triumph of virtue should treat its opponents as depraved. 'Until this faction [the Girondins] is crushed and utterly destroyed, no man can be safely virtuous', claims Robespierre.[9] In the case of a revolution whose only purpose is to hasten the inevitable victory of the proletariat, moral condemnation of enemies seems, in contrast, superfluous.

Whenever he mounted the rostrum, an orator of the French revolution had the feeling that he could change the course of events by his eloquence. He could revive courage and rally spirits. He had therefore to choose striking words, images which took hold of the mind and examples which moved his audience. Of course this search for eloquence soon became excessive and ended often in a style which looked like caricature.[10] Newspeak is very different, for this reason: its only purpose is to establish conformity with a predetermined ideological wisdom.

Deputy Petit accused the Jacobins of having made words hypocritical and untrustworthy, of always permitting a discrepancy between their words and their acts; using language to cover up violence and justify lawlessness – in other words, of corrupting the language. The same can be said of ideological speech but if one overemphasizes Newspeak as a lie-machine, one will thereby be treating it as a language, when it is no longer one at all. That is the essential point. The Jacobins did not create a new idiom. The aggressive charge which they put into their language led to a bloated and misshapen style, but it did not change the French language into something else.

PROTO-NEWSPEAK

Revolutionary brutality, then, is not enough in itself to destroy natural language: the transformation into ideological language can only take place in a language which has already been weakened.

The preliminary assault on natural language in Russia can be precisely identified because it was accurately observed at the time. It happened from 1835 onwards when young educated Russians became infatuated with German philosophy, especially that of Hegel. This infatuation developed with an almost unimaginable intensity. As many witnesses relate, Hegelianism swamped the entire cultured classes and raced through the literary reviews and the salons like wildfire. Alexander Herzen describes Hegelianism, with a certain irony, in his memoirs, emphasizing the linguistic consequences of the Hegelian frenzy which prevailed at the time:

> Young philosophers (...) took over a conventional language. They did not translate it into Russian, but because it was simpler, they transferred each word separately, often leaving Latin words in the original and merely adding the usual inflections of the seven Russian cases.

I can say this, because I was caught up in the general tide myself and wrote exactly in the same way. I was even astonished that the famous astronomer Perevoschikov called it 'bird-language'. Nobody at that time would have been troubled by a sentence like this: 'The concretization of abstract ideas in the plastic sphere implements this phase during which the mind seeks itself while attaining its own self-determination in which it potentializes itself outside the natural immanence in the harmonious sphere of consciousness which is formed in the ideal....

The fatal defect of German philosophy was that it contented itself with an artificial language, which was both heavy and scholastic, precisely because it was alive only in learned academies; in other words, in the monasteries of idealism. It is the language of the Popes of philosophy, intended for the faithful (...). Like all coded messages, one needs a key to read it (...). Feuerbach was the first to use a more accessible language (...).

Beside the corrupt language there was another, and greater, error. The young philosophers had damaged not only their language but also their judgement. Their views on life and reality became academic and 'bookish'. It was this learned view of simple things that Goethe brilliantly satirized in the discussion between the student and Mephistopheles. Everything that was real and immediate, and all simple emotions, were raised to the level of abstract categories, becoming pale, algebraic shadows without a drop of hot blood in them (...). Anyone who went for a stroll at Sokolniki went to surrender himself to the pantheistic feeling of unity with the Cosmos. If, on the way, he happened to meet a drunken soldier or a gossiping woman, the philosopher would not simply chat to them but set himself to identify the folk-substance behind their immediate and contingent forms (...).[11]

Kireevski's comments are in the same vein:

Philosophical concepts are widespread among us. Absolutely nobody converses without using philosophical terms. You will find no adolescent who does not pass judgment on

Hegel .... Even 10-year olds talk of 'concrete objectivity'.[12]

'Hegelomania' also invaded the universities, as Chicherin illustrates in his description of the Professor of Law, Redkin:

> Redkin was a man of little talent or ability. He was totally committed to the philosophy of Hegel, but, not being able to express an abstract idea clearly, he often lapsed into extreme formalism. For him, it was essential to give every principle three stages of development; and as each stage had in its turn to be subdivided into another three stages he finished up with a complicated structure, often without any content, and completely bewildering to young minds.[13]

The Press and the literature of the time freely mocked the excesses which resulted from the general infatuation with Hegel. The review *Otechestvennye Zapiski* published a satirical description of the spire of the Admirality in St Petersburg in Hegelian terms:

> Taken by itself, as an exteriorisation of the particular idea in its infinite/finite essence, it cannot be understood as a stage of development for itself and in itself, and hence as a process; or as the contemporary expression of an individual creation which concentrates itself in one point by virtue of the tendency of the objective circumference to move towards the subjective centre. Therefore it becomes, as it were, the tension of a living, whole, organism.[14]

The young Russian intelligentsia of the 'forties grew up, then, under the shadow of a philosophical jargon. Membership required acceptance of the jargon, although most of these young people had not read Hegel. For example the famous critic Belinski did not know any foreign language and had recourse to summaries of Hegel's teaching which his friends obligingly wrote for him. Even among those who had read Hegel, few understood him. They took from him a whole battery of terms which attracted them because they seemed able to encompass all reality. Vocables such as 'objective', 'subjective', 'concrete', 'abstract', 'exteriorisation', 'unilateral', 'multilateral', 'content', 'form', 'organic', 'transition' still evoke a response in the mind even when they have long ceased to be shaped by Hegel's powerful intuition; in other words, when they have ceased to be ideas at all.

For young Russians at that time, Hegel's vocabulary seemed to fulfil the promises that Schelling's *Natural Philosophy* had made in such glowing terms but failed to realise. Hegelianism provided a master-key with which to open at will all the doors of Nature, Thought and History. It was natural, therefore, that Hegel should have exercised an irresistible attraction in a country where philosophy had only just been discovered, like some New World, and where concepts had been previously nameless.[15]

> We wanted to believe in the possibility of an absolute theory which would enable us to create (or 'build', as we would say) all natural phenomena, just as we believe now in the possibility of a social order which can satisfy all human needs.[16]

In these words Odoevski, a follower of Schelling, summed up the intellectual climate of that period.

All the factors just listed – philosophical ingenuity, the lack of a tradition of abstract thought, the fascination exercised by teachings which proclaimed the unity and total intelligibility of the world, and the vulnerability of a language new to abstract terms – explain why, in Russian, words detached themselves durably from reality without at the same time developing into concepts. The eruption of philosophical jargon into society itself brought about the separation of words and things, without which the substitution of Newspeak for natural language would never have taken place. Paradoxically, the monopolistic pre-eminence of this abstract vocabulary – of what Samarine called 'the flexible schema'[17] – makes reality inaccessible to intelligence. The world of phenomena becomes impenetrable and incomprehensible – hidden behind the opposing polarities inherited from Schelling, behind negations and negations of negations, masked by exteriorisations of absolute Mind, by all kinds of 'development', by different sorts of transitions and necessary stages and by provisional objectivations, all drawn from Hegel. The individual mind ends up as if paralysed by the plethora of words imposed on it.

At first, Russians found philosophy so exhilarating that the gap between the impressive verbal machinery and the reality to which it was supposed to give access went unnoticed. 'Our authors philosophize at random (...) and (...) starting with different fragmented concepts, as in a multi-coloured kaleidoscope, they turn themes round and amuse themselves with the new combinations' wrote Belinski.[18] This was the period of 'reconciliation with reality' which Belinski and Bakunin glorified. Following Hegel, the real was declared to be the rational, but, and this was the point, the real was thereby covertly reduced to an abstraction. And it was forgotten that the philosophical systems applied only to shadows. Everything was so beautifully clear for the very reason that the mind was only manipulating its own creations instead of weighing them against an independent world.

It was an argument that had very little to do with philosophy which abruptly put an end to all that spiritual bliss, and to the dominant fashion for philosophy in Russia. People became suddenly aware that Hegel's theories were powerless to account for the notorious absurdity of serfdom and for the monstrosity that was the Russian state. Belinski and Bakunin were offended and turned away from philosophy altogether. They did not, however, give up all the mental bits and pieces of Hegelianism. For their thinking needed the framework it was accustomed to and which enabled it to find expression. It turned out, however, that these philosophical categories were not capable of defining reality; so they were referred only to what ought to be, where success was guaranteed because in that field, stubborn reality never rose to question the perfect working of abstract systems. The true place of this 'ought to be' is naturally human society, the wished for transformation of Nature being left for the scientists. So there arose the idea of 'praxis', a course of action destined to create a great future. Philosophy then turned for ever into ideology, and Newspeak took over. Hegel's dialectic became 'the mathematics of the revolution.'[19] Hegel was re-assessed and corrected by Hegelians of the left, who dismissed the content of his philosophy, and declared his system unacceptably reactionary, while fully retaining his method because, unknown to the Master, it was capable of eminently 'progressive' applications.

Certain texts show clearly how this transfer works and how the *langue de bois* slides into the gap which Hegelian terminology produced between language and reality. Belinski is a vivid example of how the Hegelian categories can have an inner hold over a man, even when he has broken with philosophy. To begin with, here is an example of how he introduces the machinery of Hegelianism into his prose.

There is only thought: beyond thought there is nothing. Thought is action and all action presupposes self-movement. Thought consists in a dialectical movement, that is to say in the spontaneous development of thought from the starting point of itself. Movement, or development, is the life and the essence of thought (...).[20]

And so the dialectical machinery was started up and hitched up to the destiny of Russia: in the following passage we see it being re-adjusted to what it ought to be:-

The vocation of Russia is to take in every living element of the whole world (...). Of course, the absorption of the universal elements of life must not, and cannot, be done mechanically (...) but in a living, organic, concrete way. Once these elements are welcomed in our experience, they will not remain there as something external and foreign: they will be transformed; this will change their nature and receive a new and original character (...). We Russians (...) are going to take over as our own property everything that is unique in the life of each European people. And we are going to take it over not as something exclusive or comprehensive but only as one element in the composition of our life, the unique aspect of which will be not abstract but concrete.[21]

This extract includes many opposed terms, one of which is approved at the expense of the other – oppositions which support a false way of thinking. This characteristic of Belinski's style is the harbinger of Newspeak. It is interesting also because it reveals one of the reasons for the extraordinary success in Russia of the Hegelian vulgate, which provided a welcome fillip to national pride after the snubs administered by Chadaev and Custine. It was re-assuring to invest in the future, since in Russia the past and the present provided so few titles to glory. Russia offered a space where all kinds of syntheses could occur, one more flattering than the other: it could reconcile the East and the West; having experienced powerful negations, the synthesis would be the most complete embodiment of Absolute Mind. Moreover, the Orthodox Church would unite the static nature of Catholicism and the dynamic quality of Protestantism: it was strongly hoped that Absolute Mind, having harvested here and there among the different European peoples, was going to take up his permanent abode in Russia. Not surprisingly the Russians welcomed the idea which Engels put forward, of separating the Hegelian method from the Hegelian system. It enabled people to use dialectic to justify the most scatterbrained proposals. As Belinski wrote:

In the end, Hegel's philosophy encompassed all the problems of the world. If his solutions were sometimes more appropriate to a bygone stage of mankind, his profound and rigorous method had nevertheless cleared the way to the understanding of human reason .... Hegel was only mistaken in his applications when he departed from his own method.[22]

For the intelligentsia, all dressed up in the dialectic, the world became absolutely unintelligible and indescribable. This frustration led them to harbour a persistent grievance against reality; eventually the *intelligent* were to demand that reason should be transformed into action so that they could finally conquer the unbearable nonsense of real things. Belinski's pathetic appeals to 'life' and 'reality' were evidence that something was missing; Arnold Ruge, a Hegelian of the left, knew the cure:-

But when we turn ourselves in the other direction, towards the irrationality of reality, we feel a lack of satisfaction, an uneasiness and an inescapable need and obligation for the praxis. Something must be done. Reason must be given its due (...). The only real thinking is in the will (...). Speculation is self-satisfied, comparing spiritual reality with external reality is not to show their difference but their identity (...). Consciousness has fundamentally changed. Progress is no longer abstract, time is politicised, even though more is needed to satisfy the mind.[23]

The Polish Hegelian, Cieszkowski, who was very popular in Russia, wrote in the same vein, using a Hegelian three-stage argument with which to bury Hegel. The ancient world was the home of feeling; the Christian world is the home of reason; the world of the future will be the home of action. The following example of his prose shows that Newspeak is not very far away:

> The future destiny of philosophy in general is to become practical, to have a concrete influence on life and society and to develop truth by means of concrete action. Philosophy's normative influence on human social relationship is beginning to operate now, so that objective truth will be seen, not only in present reality, but in the reality which is coming.[24]

Even Stankevich, whom Herzen treated as a harmless gentle dreamer, is convinced:

> The essence of the absolute is a self-evident idea: once we grasp the idea we have no need for any further knowledge, but first we must be shown that life-giving idea in itself (...). Without this struggle to comprehend it the idea becomes self-contemplation or bliss. Knowledge has disappeared. But from the idea one can build life, that is to say the idea can be made to become action (...). Knowledge itself must become action and disappear into it.[25]

A little while later, in his famous article of 1842, 'Reaction in Germany',Bakunin deduced from the Hegelian categories of opposition and contradiction that the old world must be destroyed:

By its nature and its principle the democratic party is something universal and all-comprising, but by existing as a party it stands for something specific, namely, as the negative. The reason for the negative and its insuperable strength is the destruction of the positive. But by annihilating the positive the negative meets its own end as if it were something bad, something specific which in its being is not capable of sustaining its essence. Democracy does not yet exist in a richly affirmative mode but only as the negation of the positive; and because of that it must die with the positive in order to be born again and regenerated for a rich, full life of its own.[26]

The publishing of this article, one could say, marked the end of the first stage of the formation of Newspeak. Not only are the words now cut off from any external meaning, they also claim to lay down a law for reality. However, Bakunin does not hesitate to claim that his aims derive from the category of logic; for that reason one can speak only of a proto-Newspeak. The actual is simply ignored; it is not called in to justify the imperatives of what ought to be.

THE DEFINITIVE CHANGE

Around 1850 Newspeak grew to maturity and natural science replaced metaphysics as the *dernier cri* of Russian intellectual fashion. From then on, the order of nature is referred to in absolutely every context. This does not mean that the Hegelian machinery is abandoned; the Russians, simply proceeded, in Guy Planty-Bonjour's words to 'naturalise' the dialectic. Newspeak crystallized around a double certainty.

The first certainty followed directly from Hegel's doctrine: this is the belief that the stage most recently reached by thought is also the stage of its greatest perfection. From the pedestal of modernity, one could look back condescendingly on past ages and pity the stammerings of our ancestors. A feeling was abroad that the last piece of the puzzle had been grasped and there was nothing more to be learnt. All that remained was to look for further conclusive evidence for the principles which had been discovered. This certainty partly explains the incredible self-assurance of Newspeak, and its unruffled and peremptory way of piling up affirmations while implying that only a fool or a knave could have any doubts about them.

The second source of certainty is the 'scientific alibi'. Newspeak claims to reflect the laws of matter: another reason why it allows no criticism. Natural reason is one and universal, nothing must escape it: the natural order makes the dialectic irrefutable. Here, in a curious way, Hegelian teleology intersects with a rationalism reminiscent of the 18th century; and the clash between them passes unnoticed. So now two things are necessary: the development of reason in things and societies; and the imperative adaptation of human order to the order of nature.

The review *The Contemporary* is the organ of this new tendency in Russia. In its columns from the end of the 1840's, we can find articles written in pure Newspeak. The following extract shows the resurgence of Enlightenment-type rationalism. The author is a left-wing Hegelian economist. In an article in *The Contemporary* in 1847 he criticized Malthus, blaming him, among other things for emphasizing the deep absurdity of nature. The Soviet manner already shows through, as the reader will duly notice:-

One of the most strongly held and widespread convictions of our times is that of the inflexible all-prevailing rationality of nature, its constant and infallible faithfulness to itself and of the submission of everything that exists to unique and common laws, which bring harmony and order to all physical and moral phenomena. Nowadays everyone is convinced that nature arranges everything, with foresight, as it were, and that what governs everything is not blind chance, or foolish fate, but rational necessity directing everything that seems contingent and arbitrary to one final end. This truth lies more deeply in our consciousness than any other and provides the starting point for all scientific research, all knowledge and all belief. This hypothesis of a single rationale governing the whole world was first prop-osed by Anaxagoras and later adopted by all other philosophers, who made it the basis of their systems. As the natural and historical sciences developed, this idea, which had originally been presented as an *a priori* hypothesis, became more and more unquestionable and was confirmed

by precise and dependable evidence. The more deeply the
human mind probed physical nature and the more it dwelt
attentively on the phenomena which occupy the sphere of
human activity, the more convinced it became of the
profound rationality of nature and of the coherence and
unity of its laws.[27]

Here we find together all the characteristics of Newspeak
that were brought out in the first chapter – a pronounced
tendency towards excessive noun-use, a wealth of comparatives, the absence of the author, the confusion between the
indicative and the (implied) imperative. The tone is
categorical, the words repetitive, clichés come easily and
the pathos is obvious. Newspeak has arrived and all that
remains is to discover its many resources.

An odd article by Chernichevsky brilliantly explains how
the dialectic makes it possible to adapt human life to the
laws of the physical world so as to highlight the uniformity
of universal development. This is Chernichevsky's vindica-
tion of rural communes, entitled: 'A Critique of philosophical prejudices against rural communes'. When this
article was published in 1859 it caused a great stir in Russia.
It still deserves attention, first because it is a remarkable
example of cast-iron ideological reasoning as well as being
an almost perfect instance of Newspeak. Secondly, because,
as we shall see, the argumentation is not unamusing.
Certainly, we are not used to finding such daring excursions
into geology and biology in the Newspeak of Soviet
Socialism. Chernichevsky will stop at absolutely nothing to
defeat his opponents:-

There is hardly one critic of the rural commune who does
not say, in chorus with all the others: 'The rural commune is
a primitive form of agrarian social structure while private
land-ownership represents the more developed form. How
can one not prefer a superior form to an inferior form?'
(...).

The opponents of the rural commune (...) correctly demonstrate an aspect of it which should recommend it decisively to all those who are familiar with the discoveries of German philosophy about the succession of forms within the process of universal development. How can these critics not notice that the argument against the rural commune which they adduce demonstrates the contrary, namely the correctness of the opposite opinion which prefers the rural commune to the system of private ownership (which the critics are defending)?

The highest degree of development is similar in form to the initial stage, as we see in all spheres of life. Take first the commonest form of the beginnings of life on our planet. Bodies in the liquid and gaseous state are the starting point from which our planet and the life on it have evolved. The condensation of the gas and the hardening of the liquid into various sorts of minerals were a great step forward. Stones and precious metals are the culmination of the planetary process in this direction.

Compare the age-old indestructibility and extraordinary solidity of gold and platinum to the even greater indestructibility and terrible solidity of rubies and diamonds with the instability of form and rapid processes of chemical change in gases and liquids and you will see two opposed extremes.

But then what happens? Is nature exhausted when it has become solid, dense and extremely immobile within the mineral kingdom? No, from the mineral kingdom there gradually evolves the vegetable kingdom. In a single step nature distances itself from the terrible density of minerals and returns towards the lesser density of liquids (...). The basic material of the tree (...) is united with a considerable mass of matter in a liquid state and the tree fills up with sap, which constitutes its life-giving principle. The tree inherits from the mineral immobility its own immobility of position (...). The exterior shape of the tree is also hard (...).

Then nature moves into another phase of development and after the vegetable kingdom it produces the animal kingdom. Once again it goes back to forms of life which existed before minerals. Liquid elements occupy a much greater place in animal organisms than in plants, some of them separate out independently to occupy the veins, the heart, the stomach and other reservoirs of the animal organism (...). But it is not only liquids that replace the hardness of minerals in the central organs: gases also penetrate, so that the animal organism is full of air, which concentrates fairly massively in the two principal life-sustaining organs, the lungs and the stomach (...).

What then is the difference between superior and inferior forms of organisms? In man the nervous system and most of all the brain are much more developed. And what is this mass, the development of which fulfils the highest ambitions of nature? The brain mass has an indefinite shape (...). This living jelly has an outline only because it is contained within a wall of bone. Once released from those walls, it spreads like a globule of liquid mud. The most typical element in the brain's make-up is phosphorous, which tends to revert to the gaseous state. So the crowning achievement of animal life, the highest stage of nature's processes, the nervous system, consists in the movement of brain-tissue back towards the gaseous state. Life returns to a state in which it is dominated by gas; a state which was the starting point for the development of the planet (...).

Let us move on from the processes of the earth and look at the relationship of forms in spheres closer to us. First, let us consider the character of animal life at its different stages of development. We have already stated that the highest achievement of that life, the cerebral mass, has an appearance which suggests an almost shapeless jelly, deprived of forms and qualities typical of the meaty tissues which form the dominant element of the animal world. The lower levels of animal life, which appear in molluscs and slugs, have exactly the same characteristics. The flesh of an oyster has a jelly-like appearance which is more like the brain than meat is. Thus we see once more three forms, the highest form (the brain) can be seen as a return by the second (meat) to the primitive form (gelatinous matter).[28]

It is not surprising that Lenin should have regarded Chernichevsky as his teacher. For he learned from him how evidence from the material world could be harnessed by the dialectic so as to make it the driving force of ideology. This extract shows not only the grammatical and lexical characteristics of Newspeak. It has also borrowed from Newspeak its mystique of scientific stocktaking, its determination not to spare us any detail, and its deadly tautological ponderousness. All of this shows how the dialectic shuts the mind into a closed circuit and denies it access to the specific qualities of phenomena.

The idea of development provides a pretext for the repeated affirmation of the Same – it is not for nothing that Schelling is invoked at the beginning of the extract, as well as Hegel. In the same way Soviet language will make felicitous use of the process of universal development in order to keep harking back to the Identical while avoiding the question of being.

The tone of the article is as striking as its content. The assurance of the half-educated pedant is shot through with aggression and arrogance. The quasi-scientific vocabulary serves not just to support the pretensions of intellectual upstarts like Chernichevsky and his friends at *The Contemporary*; like a battery of artillery it is also there to wipe out the enemy. Soviet language has not forgotten this device and, like Chernichevsky, uses pedantry as a means of intellectual terrorism. The dialectic becomes truly autocratic only when it is 'naturalized', that is to say, illustrated by scientific 'facts'.

One may attribute the success of Chernichevsky and his followers to three factors. First, they beguiled the public by the facility of their thought, in which the methodology of German philosophy is rendered in the simplest of words, but without any abatement of its claim to universality. Second, they presented their ideas as the consummation of universal thought, the dénouement towards which all the great doctrines of the past have been moving, at best unsuccessfully, in the face of unfavourable historical circumstances. Lastly the group grounded its doctrine on natural science from the findings of which there is no appeal. These three factors won the day. The Russian public, then composed of half-educated intellectuals, was

jealous of the elegant but inimitable language of Pushkin
and Turgenev – representatives of the preceeding aristocra-
tic generation – and so took to Newspeak like ducks to
water.

But to return to *The Contemporary*; Chernichevsky's
article on the rural commune shows us how pseudo-
Hegelianism was schematized. What follows shows Chernichevsky writing about Lessing in indulgent, condescend-
ing mood. He excuses Lessing's limitations on the grounds
of the intellectual narrowness of his times; at the same time
he pays tribute to his genius and to the important step
forward involved in moving from philosophy and theology
to social issues.

> Lessing addressed himself to those things which the public
> of his day found most interesting and intelligible. It was a
> public with a very restricted and meagre intellectual life. He
> used all the means he had to expand that life gradually, to
> make it more active and to lead it from one interest to
> another which was more important and more actual. Lessing
> died suddenly, at the beginning of one of his new creative
> stages and we can see how at each fresh start his writing
> became more vigorous and his genius expanded. His
> powerful mind took hold of themes with ever greater clarity
> and completeness, so that the object of his studies became
> ever nobler and more important. Where his development
> would have stopped, no one can know. We know only that
> he died when his thinking was still increasing in power; there
> is no evidence to show that anyone of the questions he had
> resolved up to then had exhausted his energy or satisfied his
> criteria.[29]

Because Bacon paved the way, allowance is to be made in
his case too for mitigating circumstances:

Scholasticism directly influenced pedagogy, as Francis

Bacon had already observed in the 16th century. Of course, the great philosopher was still contaminated to a considerable degree by the main prejudices of his time and could not adequately formulate what we can formulate now. But the realists who have followed him have come to a clearer and deeper understanding of things.[30]

Those two extracts could have been taken directly from the Soviet press. They display the same barbaric attitude to culture, the same cavalier criticisms of someone else's work measured by the standard of the latest ideology. Moreover the staff of *The Contemporary* owed its influence on the public also to its knack of stating platitudes in a seemingly learned language. The next two examples of Chernichevsky's platitudes would not disgrace the Soviet press:

In every society which is organized correctly and rationally, in other words, where the means of production are not left to chance or violence but arranged with foresight and reason, there must be a strong bond, a balance and a solidarity between all the different industrial sectors. The success of each of these industrial sectors is determined by the success and health of all the other sectors which by their very nature are linked in a living, organic union. That is why, if work is correctly and harmoniously organized, but under the influence of some circumstance, results in slowing down the progress of industry which supplies the needs of society, this defect in one sector of production will necessarily affect each of the other sectors as well as the economy as a whole. It is therefore completely futile to fragment something which by its nature is a unity and to consider one part of a whole in isolation from the others, when each is in a relation of absolute dependency on the whole.[31]

Note the false logic of this passage. Miliutin sees the risk of paralysis in a society with a planned economy, but uses the danger as an argument in favour of a global 'rational organization'. Thus the positive essence of the system is assumed to transcend its negative results. Like so many Soviet hacks, the same writer pushes at open doors with unshakeable calm:

'Man does not live by bread alone' says the Evangelist. The economic sense of this text lies in the fact that apart from food there exists a number of things essential to the maintenance of human life. Man's needs are varied and numerous and among them are many, which have to be satisfied just as much as nourishment. In a cold climate, clothing and housing are as necessary for man's existence as bread itself.[32]

In Russia Hegelian jargon initiated a break with ordinary language – a break that could have been as short-lived as the jargon itself. It became definitive with *The Contemporary* because the empty pseudo-Hegelian schema was given new life by false analogies and bogus science. The severance of language from reality was no longer noticed. In place of metaphysics there was evidence: instead of the painfully thought-out abstractions of preceding generations, there were ready-made ideas tailored to fit every concrete cirumstance. The reality involved was no longer the pathetic dream of Belinski but a dazzling series of facts testified to by the material world; and these facts provided a useful content for the machine of ideology.

The language of Chernichevsky made people forget that natural objects and works of culture have their *own* proper significance. His claim to universality hides his inability to grasp any specific object. This claim does not arise from a naive, youthful enthusiasm for philosophy, as was the case with the preceding generation. Rather it indicates an aggressive will to polemic: a disposition which left nothing to chance and strove relentlessly to encompass the whole world and make of it a weapon that would crush the enemy. This polemical urge brought about the break with reality as much as did the spurious and arbitrary 'evidence' from nature. A discourse that is mined with imperatives is not properly subject to the criterion of truth, even if it claims to be. Chernichevsky evokes the actual world only so as to show what it ought to be. The craving for reality which Belinski and his friends felt so strongly, even at the height of their Hegelian frenzy, is with Chernichevsky stifled by the tyranny of Utopianism.

From the 1850's onwards, thereforc, and well before Marx had made any impact on Russia, Newspeak was ready for its role, fully proof against reality; a superb instrument for the power-struggle and for the rape of the mind. Newspeak was ready for use by anyone who could see its advantages and its potential. In the 1890's the intellectual terrorism set up by *The Contemporary* went into decline, but the *langue de bois* which that review propagated had had time to fulfil its task of forming the 'new man', of inculcating in him the intellectual dishonesty, the indifference to truth, and all the opportunism and arrogance that comes from being dead certain that one is right.

NEWSPEAK AND MARXISM

Marxism breathed new energy into Newspeak and brought it into full possession of its faculties. Chernichevsky's teaching contained a flaw. His simplistic 'scientism' put him at risk of being caught out in a downright lie; for the reality he referred to, however immersed in the torrent of dialectic, depended on the existence of stable forms at least at each stage of development. Unwisely, he committed himself to a concept of matter as something which solidified in stages and to a psychology based on a flat-footed naturalism which excluded history. In short, although he was an ardent disciple of development-theory, Chernichevsky was undermined without his realizing it by concepts inherited from the 18th century. He had not decided to do away with nature, even at the heart of humanity: he compounded his error by seeing it as the final argument, the source of certainty, something never to be reduced. So his Newspeak remained naive and vulnerable compared to *langue de bois* of Marxism. For though Chernichevsky had so freely denied, by means of the dialectic, the specificity of phenomena, he was in perpetual danger of colliding with the very nature to which he made such appeal. In other words he was never sheltered from the threat of the truth.

All this contrasts sharply with Marxist Newspeak, which

can be spread everywhere in complete safety. Truth will never pick a quarrel with this language, because Marxist truth is in a permanent state of fabrication. Based on material reality as conceived by Marx, Newspeak is in no danger from an untimely irruption of ontology, for its reality is that of 'concrete human activity' – 'praxis'. All phenomena hide something else, nothing stands for itself and everything is the product of some activity. The whole of nature is indeed eliminated, though without in any way giving up the benefit of a positive and undeniable content. Hegel's system can now be applied without difficulty to a matter made in its own image. Thus language does not have to mean anything, since things in themselves already make sense. Ideological discourse must unravel meaning while losing no time in giving things a name. Words no longer need to refer, only to interpret. The outcome reflects the forces which made it; consciousness reflects the 'process of material life' from which it originates; and the world of the senses is based on 'the unceasing material creation of men'.[32] Marx himself did not write in *langue de bois*; but it is easy to see how his theories gave that language fresh impetus and assured it a brilliant future. The sort of certainty they provide is vastly preferable to the childish scientism of Chernichevsky and they cannot be refuted since they are based on a reality which is in perpetual change – a change, moreover, which depends on the human will. Their content retains its authority; but it no longer concerns what is, and what can therefore oppose its inert mass of reality to what ought to be: it has become the support of praxis. Scientific method seems at last to be reconciled with the imperative mood, and knowledge to be inextricably bound up with action. History is now on our side: we can predict it and further it thanks to our understanding, whereas according to Hegel we had to be content with knowing it *a posteriori*. And we have access to an unanswerable wisdom, which transforms everything it touches.

The perfect fusion of Marxist ideology and the *langue de bois*[34] derives essentially from three factors. First, they have a common origin in left-wing Hegelianism. Second, they are drawn together by their polemic mission – Marxism provides Newspeak with an arsenal beyond the wildest dreams of Chernichevsky. What adversary could resist the combined onslaught of science, matter and history as conjointly systematized by Marx?

Finally, Marxist ideology has been able to deprive phenomena of their autonomy. Hence its predilection for a language in which concepts are de-stabilized and representations avoided. The mind more easily ascends to the principle behind phenomena if it is not hampered by external references or fixed by a concept.

The language of Chernichevsky suffered no change in its structure or vocabulary in becoming Marxist, but Marxism has permanently insulated Newspeak from the influence of ordinary language and put it into the orbit of make-believe, where it can circle for ever.

LENINIST NEWSPEAK

Armed by Marxism, Newspeak was able to abandon its role as an instrument of purely theoretical polemic and become instead an instrument of political struggle. Plekhanov and Lenin did nothing to change the essential nature of Newspeak. Lenin's originality lay in his awareness of the use he could make of it in the conquest of power-struggle and the safeguarding of the new regime. With Lenin, Newspeak becomes truly an instrument.

It is amusing to watch Western Marxist researchers thrown into disarray by the philosophical writings of Lenin. They are ruefully surprised at his 'misunderstandings' and display the utmost ingenuity in excusing his idiocies[35], without appreciating that Lenin always sought, in his usual dogged spirit, a quite precise objective – to transcribe philosophy into Newspeak. He did so in order to make it a useful instrument in the struggle against 'opportunists' of all kinds. Lenin's whole effort was to extract from the body of philosophy a certain number of boss-words which could be used as rallying cries or, still more importantly, as expressions of hatred. In his *Philosophical Notebooks* he undertook to transpose, for his own personal use, the *Science of Logic* into Newspeak. The following example shows his philosophical method. Hegel wrote: 'Logic is pure science, that is to say, pure knowledge in the fullness of its development.' Lenin's comment was: 'The first part is ridiculous, the second is first-class.' The word 'development' is so charged with positive overtones and lights up to clearly the area occupied by ideology that it aroused Lenin's enthusiasm simply by being there. Obviously the search for meaning was the least of Lenin's worries. For him, philosophy was to be reduced to a set of signals which would help him test the reactions of potential disciples and to select those who were worthy of joining the brotherhood of 'new men' and those who were not.

This *langue de bois*, loaded with the cast-offs of philosophy, played a fundamental role in the constitution of the Bolshevik party. By means of successive expulsions Lenin succeeded in creating a new sort of Party, which stressed absolute obedience rather than numerical size. Lenin did not use language to convince men, but rather in order to sort them into sheep and goats, swans and geese. Language made some of them into his instruments, others into his enemies. For Lenin, language was a way of identifying and silencing the enemy and of guaranteeing the cohesion of a party which was, from the first, outside civil society and its interests. At a critical moment for himself and his party, Lenin owed his survival and that of the Bolsheviks to Newspeak. The Bolsheviks were caught unprepared by the February Revolution. Some were tempted to collaborate with various 'reformists' and to become a parliamentary opposition of the extreme Left. From February on, Lenin sensed this danger and bombarded his friends with letters ordering them not to give 'the slightest support or comfort to the new Government'[36] and advising them to wait and to 'make armed preparations for a base from which they could move to a higher revolutionary stage'.[37] To Irès Armand, he wrote:

'(....) We must not make a fetish of the Revolution.
Kerensky is a revolutionary, but he is a garrulous liar who is
deceiving the workers.[38]

For the use of the masses, he wrote a description of the
Provisional Government which anticipates, line for line, the
image of Polish Solidarity released to the Soviet public by
the official Press. The February Revolution, he thundered,
was a plot organized abroad; its leaders were the willing
puppets of imperialism:

> This week-long Revolution was 'acted out', if one is allowed
> to describe it in metaphor, after about ten major and minor
> rehearsals. The 'actors' know one another and they know
> their roles, their cues and their places up, down and
> sideways. They know every nuance, however insignificant,
> of their political leanings and how to enact them (...).
> English and French imperialist capital, for the sake of
> continuing and worsening the massacre, have plotted the
> intrigues in the Palace with officers of the Guard; have
> incited and encouraged the Gutchkovs and Milivkovs and
> recruited a new government ready to take over power after
> the opening rounds of the struggle of the proletariat against
> Tsarism.[39]

Lenin's polemical tactic is always the same. He describes
his adversaries as grotesque and hateful monsters. He loads
them with abuse and places them between reality and the
public, winning over the latter by the slickness of his
personification.[40] The real situation is thus lost to view and
replaced by the most shameless demagogy. Furthermore,
the targeted adversaries have practically no defence since it
is neither them nor their real views which are attacked, but
Aunt Sallies which have nothing to do with them. Anything
they can say is discredited in advance and, at the end of the

day, lacks all interest. Only the corrupt principle imputed to them has any emotive significance.

This crude tactic is effective, because it paralyses the enemy, makes him multiply concessions in order to show that he is not adamantly against negotiation, and finally convinces him that he should yield without a fight. Bolshevik propaganda draws the enemy onto its own ground where it has no difficulty in defeating him. The fate of the Provisional Government is the first example of the extraordinary dominance of Leninist speech. But there have been other such examples, and not only in the Soviet Union. The Western Communist Parties fascinate intellectuals with their basilisk stare, largely because of the common powerlessness to awaken from the nightmare of Newspeak.

After he took power, Lenin had more to do than expel undesirable elements. He had to give an ideologically acceptable explanation of the disasters which followed the victory of Communism. It became essential to pin-point and identify the causes of the country's setbacks so as to hide the fact that resistance to communism existed everywhere and that the very existence of civil society is a counter-revolutionary phenomenon. While denouncing the men of ill will who were frustrating the emergence of the new world, he hastened to proclaim the closeness of Utopia and the easy ways which led to it.

Right up to his death, Lenin tirelessly repeated his abuse and his exhortations; pathos invades all his speeches and writings.[41] A sort of religious terminology appeared in his speeches, revealing the intensity of his ideological will: 'Every pound of bread and fuel is truly a sacred object (...). The mass of forward-looking workers must march in a "crusade" on the places where bread is produced (...).[42]' In the same way, expressions drawn from military terminology were introduced during the war and found a permanent niche in Newspeak. For Lenin and his successors, setbacks had to be blamed on bad execution of Party directives, due either to sabotage or incompetence. Hence his perpetual appeals to discipline and efficiency and his notorious attacks on bureaucratic red tape in which Newspeak finds an inexhaustible source of commonplaces. Frenzied exhortation to instant action indefinitely postponed a true assessment of the fiasco brought about by the 'building of Communism'. Newspeak created this spurious haste, which prevented people being pulled up short by the overwhelming evidence of facts. Perception was replaced by an all-out exercise of the will.

THE SPREAD OF NEWSPEAK AFTER THE BOLSHEVIK TAKE-OVER

Once the Soviet regime was installed, wooden language was systematically spread throughout the country. Press-freedom was abolished and, in addition, major campaigns were launched against illiteracy, which were often simply excuses for teaching Newspeak. Illiteracy was to be abolished because it was intolerable that anyone should escape propaganda.

Apart from the drive for literacy, the mania for holding meetings, rampant at that time, helped to establish Newspeak. The towns sent cohorts of speakers into the countryside, whose duty it was to explain to audiences of dumbfounded peasants the cunning plots of Franco-British imperialism and the virtues of dialectical materialism. Often these amateur orators had such a poor understanding of their subject that they simply stammered through a rehash of topical slogans, hastily piling up phrases from Newspeak onto them. However, despite the scepticism and apathy of the people who were forced to waste their time on these idiotic occasions, the sessions of *politgramota*, as it was called, did have one result. Newspeak became the means by which alphabetic people distanced themselves from the rest. Newspeak became the index of one's culture and social status. Before terror imposed the *langue de bois*, snobbery did. One could cut quite a dash by juggling with learned terms. When they were bowdlerised nobody noticed. The literature of the 'twenties is full of satires mocking this gobbledegook. Used from such human motives as vanity and the desire to please – for even lovers did their courting in Newspeak – it had become a parody before anyone set out deliberately to make it one. The writer Mikhail Zoschenko is unrivalled in reproducing this peculiar speech, which he called 'monkey language'.

The whole thing began with a trifling incident. My neighbour, a young man with a beard, leaned towards the man on his left and asked politely: 'Well, comrade, will this be a plenary session or not?'

'A plenary session', said his neighbour off-handedly.

'Really!', said the first, surprised. 'I was wondering what was happening, though it seemed it was going to be plenary.'

'You can be sure of it', said the second, seriously.

'Today it is very plenary indeed; and as they've collected a proper quorum, things are going to warm up.'

'Impossible', said my neighbour, 'have they really truly got a quorum?'

'I assure you they have,' said the second.

'What about this quorum?'

'Oh, nothing really,' said his neighbour, slightly embarrassed. 'It has met, that's all that matters.'

'It's incredible', said the first, with a worried look and shaking his head.

'What happened to it, I wonder?'

The second speaker made a puzzled gesture and looked sternly at the questioner. Then, smiling sweetly, he said:

'It could well be, comrade, that you don't approve of plenary sessions .... As for me, I don't know why I find them so congenial. Everything seems to me to be in that minimal fashion following the essential of the day .... Though, to speak frankly, I have a quite permanent relationship with these meetings. In a way, you know, the industry of the insignificant.'

'It isn't always like this', said the first.

'Certainly it depends on one's point of view. If you do look at it from the point of view, it is yes, the industry concretely.'

'Concretely in fact', the second speaker correctly sternly.

'If you like', agreed the other speaker. 'I accept that also: concretely in fact. Even though that depends ....'

'Always', *interrupted the other sharply*. '*Always*, honourable comrade. Especially if the sub-section is concocted minimally, after the speech, there's no way to avoid noisy interruptions or shouting.'

A man stepped up on the rostrum and made a signal with his hand. Everyone stopped speaking. Only my neighbours, a little heated from the dispute, went on. The first speaker could not grasp the idea that the sub-section might be concocted in a minimal way.

There were calls for order. My neighbours shrugged their shoulders and shut up. Then the first speaker leaned over again to the second and asked quietly:

'Who is speaking?'

'Him? He's the presidium of course. A very sharp-spoken man. And a first-class orator. He always makes ardent speeches on the vital issues of the day.'

The speaker spread his arms and began his speech. While he was uttering high-faluting words, whose meaning was strangely vague, my neighbours nodded in a serious, thoughtful manner. The second man looked sternly at the first, meaning to show that, in spite of everything he had been in the right in the argument that had just ended. It is difficult, comrades, to speak Russian.[43]

One can see that learning Newspeak did not come easily to a population which not long before had been illiterate. The desire not to be taken for a country bumpkin played an important part in the inculcation of *langue de bois*.

Newspeak was at first copied from mouth to mouth in a voluntary, if amateurish, fashion. This was before it was imposed by terror and had become necessary for one's personal safety. For a long time the language was not regarded as ideological and looked simply like a parody of itself. It was often used for non-ideological subjects; or stuffed with a content that inflated it to the point of explosion.

The works of the writer A. Platonov owe a lot to this break-up caused by Newspeak's being brought into contact with corrosive reality. Even Soviet Communists complain of the intrusion of 'bureaucratic' jargon, and say that they mean to restore the purity of classical Russian. Perhaps their motive in this is one of fear – fear that Newspeak will be corrupted by being used in contexts where it has a natural inferiority or in situations where it has no relevance. 'We need good editions of our classics, so that the working-class can absorb their great heritage .... We no longer know how to speak our fine old Russian language. Even now we still abuse it with this Soviet parroting' writes D. Riazanov.[44] Obviously these protestations remain no more than pious hopes, while the official language blankets more and more of the country.

PERFECTED NEWSPEAK

With the coming of Stalinism, Newspeak took over from 'monkey-language'. It was no longer a matter of producing botched imitations of the learned language found in newspapers and books. Now one was obliged to reproduce, word for word, the slogans and catch-phrases, at the risk, if one did not, of being taken for a deviationist or revisionist and possibly ending up in the Gulag.

Moreover, Newspeak was changing its complexion: it was losing its aggression – outwardly, at least – and adopting a solemn, almost serene tone. No longer would it tolerate eccentric outbursts like those of Marr, or such flashes of brilliance as those of Trotsky.

Stalin's language tries hard to keep at a distance the here and now with which Leninist discourse was obsessed. Abuse and exhortations are given much less importance, without being eliminated altogether. But the urgency which marked every speech of Lenin is no longer apparent. Under Stalin, Newspeak no longer shows that it is produced to counter a still hostile reality. Stalinese hides all the actual circumstances which give rise to it and becomes an illustration of eternity. Under Lenin, Newspeak expressed the maximalism which was necessary to ensure the cohesion of the new party. Under Stalin, it became the means of pointing out the middle way between extremes that inspire fear.

Stalin succeeded in turning the emptiness of ideology into a technique of persuasion. By setting up imaginary foils, he was able eventually to present his policy as if it were a concession to reason, and not what it was – ideology pure, simple and extreme . Newspeak enabled him to give credibility to the idea that there is a *moderate* version of ideology, infinitely preferable to the alternative 'muscular' style. Stalin's speeches brilliantly invoked the fear of the worst, a sentiment which gives stability to power. Even under Brezhnev the promises of a golden future, regularly repeated in the Press, were seen by Soviet citizens as clear threats. For the people feared above all else that the Party and the Government would embark on the extra effort necessary for the final triumph of Communism. Brezhnev cleverly exploited the role of 'moderate' or middle-of-the-roader, which he had borrowed from Stalin. Now Gorbachev follows suit, warning us against the danger of a 'return to Stalinism' (very unlikely, as no Party member is eager to risk his life) and of various 'extremisms'.

Under Stalin and his successors, then, verbal violence is less superficially apparent than in Lenin's Newspeak. The following quotation is an example of how Stalin gently rebuffed those who did not believe in gaining the support of the peasants for Socialism:

It is said that this task [building the foundations of the Socialist economy] may turn out to be beyond the strength of a peasant country like Russia. Some sceptics even went so far as to say that it was Utopian and could not be realized, because the peasantry were the peasantry, i.e. producers on a small scale and for that reason unorganizable when it came to laying the foundations of Socialist production.

But the sceptics are wrong, because they pay no heed to certain factors which, in this instance, are of decisive importance. The main ones are (...)
What do all these facts mean?

That the Sceptics are wrong.
That Leninism is right to regard the mass of working
peasants as the reserve for the proletariat.[45]

Instead of anathematising all and sundry, Stalin adopted
an apparently schoolmasterly patience, insisting on the
reassuring objectivity of facts. He seemed almost indulgent
towards the weaknesses of human reason. Brutality was no
longer on the surface of words: it was located elsewhere. It
resided in his insolent way of contradicting reality, and in
the blackmail which consisted in implying that things could
be worse. This message was implicit in Stalinist Newspeak.
Once ideological power was securely in place, Newspeak no
longer needed to pose as an answer to the appeals of the
day: such a pretence would even be dangerous for it.
Instead it can settle down in a false serenity, invulnerable to
disasters, famine, purges, wars, or the death of great
leaders, unrolling the ceremonial carpet which hides all
those things from the eyes of the people and of history.
Under Stalin and Brezhnev, Newspeak attained its peak of
perfection and it is now quite capable of surviving all shocks
and meeting all eventualities.

Stalin's successors have done nothing to alter the new
wooden language[46] and they have good reason. It has
become so completely independent, so automatic, that the
only modification left to it would be its disappearance.

NOTES ON GORBACHEV

The Gorbachev period has brought in a new phase of Newspeak. *Glasnost* affects it in two ways. First, it has injected a new dose in the form of a booster to the old polarity between 'old' and 'new'. This pair of opposites, essential to Newspeak, had been worn out by the old style of wooden language: it had become almost impossible to go on talking about the *damnosa hereditas* of Tsarism in order to justify communist disappointments. Now the antithesis is between the 'period of stagnation', 'the old methods', 'out-of-date stereotypes' on the one hand; and on the other the new era of *perestroika* which must at last reveal 'the superiority of socialism' – a superiority that had remained in suspense because of the incompetence of the Stalinist bureaucracy. The new Party-line amounts to a vigorous *reprise* of messianic bolshevism. Forgotten under Leonid Brezhnev, messianism has returned to add a new dynamism to Soviet language.

At the same time *glasnost* has accelerated the erosion of the ideology; or, more exactly, it has allowed this erosion (which began long before Gorbachev) to leave its mark on official and above all semi-official speech. Newspeak no longer monopolises the media, so that one can often find, side by side in the same newspaper, articles written in an almost natural language together with others which respect all the canons of traditional Sovspeak. One seems to experience flux and re-flux, with a stretch of natural language invariably succeeded by a wave of Newspeak. Neither seems to win the day so as to exclude the other. The oscillations between them are like echoes of turbulences which remain out of sight.

The Gorbachevian *perestroika* has put Newspeak on the defensive, as is revealed in the following features:

1) a retreat of ceremonial Newspeak, such as was familiar under Brezhnev;

2) an increase in pathos;

3) an extension of the false natural language, combined with a linguistic technique that enables Newspeak to disguise itself. The Gorbachevian glossary borrows many terms referring to public morality. It is also taking on board an unbelievable number of miscellaneous anglicisms such as 'marketing', 'image', 'briefing'.

4) A more *nuancé* approach to the problem of describing socialism's enemy, who has been christened 'enemy of *perestroika*'. The concept of the enemy continues to comprise whole social categories ('bureaucrats' who continue to 'administer in the old style'; lazy workmen who have a 'parasitic mentality'; 'corrupt cadres'; and 'speculators'). But the 'enemy' sometimes takes on political colouring, especially in the context of national conflicts. Newspeak does not want to recognise that vast crowds are now demonstrating against the communist regime. So it is careful to distinguish between 'immature elements' and people who are 'politically disorientated' on the one hand and, on the other, those who are leading them by the nose – i.e. 'extremists', 'adventurers', 'political careerists', all obviously in the pay of the CIA. As in the past, however, the evil is at the same time both highly localised and extended everywhere. The press never ceases to repeat that in every Soviet person there is to be found an enemy of

perestroika.

5) Another feature of Gorbachevian Newspeak is its systematic accent on 'the middle course' that the government is following. This line distances itself from both 'conservatives' and 'negativists' (the term for those who hold that *perestroika* brings no good to the people, and, further, that the communist system cannot be reformed). Official propaganda continually advocates 'the development of discussion' (which means the self-censorship of the discussants); 'objectivity' (which consists in recognising socialism's immense achievements instead of concentrating on its 'negative aspects'); the 'journalistic ethic' (self-censorship, again); 'constructive' criticism (namely recognition of the regime's legitimacy).

One must therefore not exaggerate the retreat of Newspeak. In a certain sense it is becoming more dangerous, now that it has reached an unprecedented degree of hypocrisy and dissimulation. The mythology of the 'enemies of *perestroika*' has captivated the West more thoroughly than that of 'the Zinovievist-Trotskyist mad dogs' of yesterday. Many people are now taken in by the fundamental lie of Gorbachevian Newspeak that fundamental change has already come, when in reality the umbilical cord with Leninism remains uncut.

Notes to Chapter V

[1] Quoted in G. Walter, *La Conjuration du Neuf Thermidor*, Gallimard, 1974, pp. 395-397.
[2] M. Robespierre, *Oeuvres*, Paris, 1866, Speech of 25 September 1794.

[3] Ibid, Speech of 28 December, 1792.

[4] Ibid, speech of 24 October, 1793.

[5] Ibid, speech of 1 February, 1794.

[6] M. Robespierre, 1866, Speech of 26 May, 1794.

[7] Ibid, Speech of 11 August, 1793.

[8] Camille Desmoulins, *Le Vieux Cordelier*, IV, Paris, 1936, p.114.

[9] Robespierre, 1866, Speech of 16 June, 1793.

[10] For example, Danton dauntlessly claimed: 'I am entrenched in the citadel of reason: I will leave it with the canon of truth.' Saint-Just used images which were no less bold: 'The sword of the law will clash with the daggers of the assassins.'

[11] A. Herzen, '*Byloe i Dumy*', in: *Collected Works* vol. XIII, St Petersburg, 1919, pp. 11 et.seq.

[12] Quoted in: A. Koyré, *Études sur l'histoire de la pensée philosophique en Russie*, Paris, 1950, p.104.

[13] B.N. Chicherin, *Memories of Moscow in the Eighteen-Forties*, Moscow 1929, p.37.

[14] Quoted in: D. Chizhevsky, *Hegel in Russia*, Paris, 1939, pp.66-67.

[15] In this connection see G. Planty-Bonjour, *Hegel et la pensée philosophique en Russie, 1830-1917*, The Hague, 1974, p.4.

[16] Quoted in: A. Walicki, *A History of Russian Thought from the Enlightenment to Marxism*, Stanford, 1979, p.76.

[17] Quoted in: G. Planty-Bonjour, 1974, p.90.

[18] V. Belinski, *Sochineya*, Moscow, 1868, p.124.

[19] A. Herzen, 1919, p.16.

[20] A. Koyré, 1950, p.149

[21] A. Koyré, 1950, p.157.

[22] Quoted in: G. Planty-Bonjour, 1974, p.53.

[23] Quoted in: A. Koyré, 1950, p.208.

[24] Ibid, p.191.

[25] N.V. Stankevich, *Notes*, 1914, p.672.

[26] Quoted in: A. Koyré, 1950, p.140.

[27] V.A. Miljutin, *Selected Works*, Moscow, 1946, p.79.

[28] N.G. Chernichevsky, 'A Critique of certain philosophical warnings against a communal system of land-ownership' in *The Contemporary* 1859, pp. 7 *et seq*. (The stiffness of our translation is due to a concern to be absolutely faithful to the original.)

29 N.G. Chernichevsky, *Collected Works*, Moscow, Vol. IV, p.215.

30 A. Sleptsov, 'Pedagogical Conversations' in *The Contemporary*, 1863, Vol. XCIV, p.297.

31 V.A. Miljutin, 1946, p.102.

32 Ibid, p.100.

33 See K. Marx & F. Engels, *The German Ideology*, Paris, 1968, pp. 556 et seq.

34 The interesting question here is what was it in Marxist ideology that invited expression in wooden language? (Obviously we are not saying that all Russian authors inspired by Marx expressed themselves in *Newspeak*).

35 See for example G. Planty-Bonjour, 1974, pp. 280 et seq.

36 V.I. Lenin, *Collected Works 3*, vol. XXXIV, p.240 'Letter to A. Kollontai' of 16 March, 1917.

37 Ibid.

38 Ibid, p.248, 'Letter to Inès Armand'.

39 Quoted in D. Shturman, *Myertvye khvatayut shyvykh: Chitaya Lenina, Bukharina, Trotskogo*, (*The Dead Seize the Living*: *Readings from Lenin, Bukharin and Trotsky*,) London, 1982, p.62.

40 D. Shturman (ibid.) gives an excellent analysis of this Leninist procedure, which consists in flourishing caricatures like puppets before the eyes of the masses.

41 D. Shturman gives a great many examples of this sort of frenzied activism which came over Lenin once the Bolsheviks were in power. Nothing mattered but to increase vigilance and efficiency, to overcome apathy etc. At no time did Lenin give a true account of the stagnation in the country. Much of these *topoi* have come back under Gorbachev.

42 Quoted in: D. Shturman, 1982, pp. 101, 102. It would be tiresome to list every term from the glossary of religion or all the archaisms which had a place in wooden language at this time. There is a list in A.M. Selishchev, 1928, pp.62 et seq.

43 Quoted in: A.M. Selishchev, 1928, pp. 57-58. Other stories by Zoschenko are on the same theme, especially one entitled 'M. Agitator', in: *Izbrannoe*, (Selections), Leningrad, 1978, pp. 84, 85.

[44] Ibid, p.56.

[45] J. Stalin, *Principles of Leninism*, Peking, 1969, pp. 65, 66.

[46] Gorbachev's Newspeak has brought some lexical innovations (emphasis on 'acceleration', 'renewal', 'deformations of social-ism', etc.). But the functioning of Newspeak as shown above remains identical. More place now is given in the press to 'ordinary speech'. But the mimicry and parasitism of Newspeak should not be overlooked: it is they that are exemplified whenever Newspeak strives to imitate moral, economic or even political discourse.

AN ANTI-LANGUAGE

It may seem odd that so many noble disciplines – grammar, rhetoric, philosophy, history – should have been pressed into service to give an account of Newspeak, the shoddy little product of ideology. But the fact is that the mind has no defence against its own impostures, especially against things which flatter its worst tendencies. This book has shown how difficult it is to pin down the essence of *langue de bois*. We had at all costs to remain outside this system of automatic thinking, this mechanical speech which hypnotizes the spirit and paralyses reason. It was therefore necessary to anchor ourselves to those old disciplines before setting out to explore this weird product of the human mind.

By doing so, we have been able to bring into the open the basic deception of Newspeak: despite appearing in the guise of words and sentences, it is no longer a language. The things that make up language – the freedom to choose words and themes, an identifiable author, indications of time, organized thought, coherent meaning – all these are absent. Once it is taken over by ideology, language becomes a shadow of itself. Even so, it is worth close study since this enables us to understand ideology itself, and how the ideological impinges on the real. Newspeak shows how an empty nothing, a sheer will to destroy, can eventually demolish something as strong as human language: the only thing in the world which is not worn out by use, indeed which grows as it is used.

Ideology has no forms of its own and must therefore adopt existing forms in order to accomplish its work of destruction. It is condemned to appear only in alien shapes. Language is an ideal receptacle for ideology since language depends so much on conventions. The arbitrary nature of the sign makes it an easy and tempting prey, a mode of incarnation which is economical, advantageous and requires the minimum of compromise. The treatment given to language once it has been subverted by ideology is the same treatment given to all the institutions and organizations hijacked by communist power. First of all the language is emptied of content, eaten from inside by a parasite which leaves intact only the fragile external envelope: then – and this is the vital point – the language becomes a destructive instrument itself. In order to be even more deadly, it splits into an open mode (the ceremonial wooden discourse) and an informal mode, that of a false natural language.

Just as the living Church created by Communists aims to destroy religion; just as dishonest elections are held to discredit democratic procedures; just as false legality seeks to pre-empt genuine law: so this counterfeit language blocks communication, holds back the formation of a civil society which could jeopardize Communist power, inveigles thought into dead ends and hampers the emergency of a personal self within *homo sovieticus*. Among all the living dead set in motion by ideology, the zombie language is the most dangerous thing of all.

It does not stop at selecting just a few targets for its ideological death-ray. Its destructive energies are much more widely directed, against the heart of thought and of consciousness. Via concepts, representation and memory, Newspeak targets the very principle of individuation, and the essence of things and beings. The dialectical movement is imposed on phenomena and concepts until intelligence crumbles. In the maze of 'developments' the mind can find no clear outlines, while the repeated affirmation of generalities detached from reality leaves no place for the individual self. Reason loses the power to make distinctions. Particular objects melt away into the formlessness of becoming. All the characteristics of Newspeak which we have noted can be inferred from its determination to abolish specifics, or rather to come between them and consciousness, for fear that they will lead the mind along non-ideological paths. Hence the substitution of value for meaning, the absence of 'shifters', the avoidance of verbs, the stress put upon processes, the suppression of the speaker in his speech and even, paradoxical as it may seem, the use of allegory. All situations, things, or men, can be reduced to a principle which transcends them. The speaker is eliminated from his speech, which plays on without him. Nothing is spared in this attack against form and time. Newspeak eliminates both memory and the sense of identity: it dismisses phenomena and concepts simultaneously. This explains the disappearance of meaning. Meaning can exist only where there is a differentiation among objects, and a distinction between object and subject.

One has still to consider the reasons for the success of Newspeak – how this monotonous and ungracious form of speech took hold of whole groups in society even before the Communist regime had officially imposed it; and how it spread beyond the frontiers of the Soviet Union into countries where it managed to exist side by side with a free Press. How do people fail to notice the damage Newspeak does to intelligence, or the lack of humanity that it induces in its victims? Finally, why is it so difficult to free oneself from Newspeak if one has been brought up on it from childhood?

The reason is that ideology and *langue de bois* corrupt both the heart and the mind, by promising them instant omnipotence, simplified thinking and ready-made discourse. In the sort of light-headedness brought on by ideology, reason moves around easily, lifts any burden without effort, and experiences that feeling of euphoria which drowning people are said to experience before their end. Thought is freed from the necessity to face up to external objects; man is given an idiom with a built-in self-generating mechanism which fuels the speaker without his having to make the least effort. To repel the temptations of ideology and put an end to the malign flow of Newspeak one must be fortified by the conviction that things can only be understood in their context; that knowledge cares little for *praxis* and that in the end whoever thinks truly must also choose his own words to formulate his thought. After the debilitating effect of ideology, the discipline of reality can seem brutal. But one has to remember that a world in which there is still much to discover is infinitely preferable to a predictable universe about which everything has already been said.

BIBLIOGRAPHY

The following is a list of books referred to in the text. Where possible we have tried to give English editions. Russian titles are given in orthodox English transcription.

N.T. Abramova, 'Filosofskie Voprosy Kibernitiki', in *Voprosy Filosofii*, no. 3, 1981.
Aristotle, *Rhetoric*.
Saint Augustine, 'De mendacio', in *Oeuvres*, II, Paris, 1937, pp. 234-305.

H. Barbusse, *Staline*, Paris 1935.
Leszek Bednargzuk, 'Wladza nad mówa', in *Pismo*, 2, April 1981, pp. 93-102.
V. Belinski, *Sochinenya*, Moscow, 1868.
V. Belov, 'Jazyk moj, drug moj' in *Nash Sovremennik*, no. 7, 1983, pp. 181-187.
E. Benveniste, *Problèmes de linguistique générale*, Paris, 1966.
Cornelia Berning, *Vom 'Abstammungsnachweis' zum 'Zuchtwart': Vokabular des Nationalisozialismus*, Berlin, 1964.
Alain Besançon, *The Intellectual Origins of Leninism*, Oxford,1981.

Alain Besançon, 'La conviction idéologique, in: *Commentaire*, Autumn 80, no. 11.

Alain Besançon, *Anatomie d'un spectre*, Paris, Calmann-Lévy, 1981.

Ladislas Bod, 'Langage et pouvoir politique: réflexions sur le stalinisme' in: *Études*, Feb. 1975, pp. 177-213.

W. J. Brazill, *The Young Hegelians*, New Haven & London, 1970.

M. Bronski, 'Totalitarny jezyk kommunizmu' in: *Kultura*, 12, 1979, pp. 91-99.

Brosses (le Président de), *Traité de la formation mécanique des langues et des principes physiques de l'étymologie*, Paris, 1765.

I. Chafarevitch, *Le Phénomène socialiste*, Paris, 1977.

N. G. Chernichevsky, 'Kritika filosofskikh predubezhdenij protiv obshchinnogo vladenija' in: *Sovremennik*, 1859.

N. G. Chernichevsky, *Collected Works*, Moscow, 1939.

B. N. Chicherin, *Vospominanija Moskva 40-kh godov*, Moscow, 1929.

Anna Chmielewska, 'Kampania', in: *Zapis*, no. 4, 1977, pp. 78-90.

Condillac, *Oeuvres choisies*, vol. I, *Grammaire*, Paris, 1796.

J. Cunningham, *The Problem of Style*, New York, 1966.

Camille Desmoulins, *Le Vieux Cordelier*, Paris, 1936.

N. Dobroljurbov, 'Literaturnye melochi proshlogo goa', in: *Sovremennik*, no. 4, 1859.

V. Erofeev, *Moskva-Petushki*, Paris, 1977.

P. N. Fedoseev, 'V. I. Lenin i filosofskie problemy sovremennogo estestvoznanija' in: *Voprosy filosofii*, no. 6, 1981.

Pierre Fontanier, *Les figures du discours*, Paris, 1968.

K. W. Fricke, 'Die Sprache des Vierten Reiches' in: *Deutsche Rundschau*, vol. 12, December 1952, pp. 1243-1246.

R. Gaudig, 'Die deutsche Sprachspaltung' in: *Neue Deutsche Hefte*, 55, Feb. 1959.

E. Gilson, *Linguistique et philosophie*, Paris, 1969.

Colin H. Good, *Die deutsche Sprache und die kommunistische Ideologie*, Frankfurt, 1975.

Marian Gorecki, 'Wzgielku dreczonych wyrazów' in: *Wezwanie*, no. 4, 1982, pp. 28-35.

H. Grunert, *Sprache und Politik*, Berlin-New York, 1974.

G. Guillaume, *Langage et science du langage*, Paris, 1964.

G. W. F. Hegel, *The Phenomenology of Spirit*, Oxford, 1978.

M. Heller, 'Jezyk sowieckai a jezyk rosyjski' in: *Kultura*, 12, 1979, pp. 99-103.

A. Herzen, 'Byloe i Dumy' in: *Collected Works*, vol. XIII, St Petersburg, 1919.

Gayle D. Hollander, *Soviet Political Indoctrination*, New York, 1972.

R. Jakobson, *Essai de linguistique générale*, Paris, 1963.

C. Jelen, *Le 'PCF' sans peine*, Paris, Fayard, 1981.

Jezyk propagandy, Warszawa, 1978.

M. I. Kalinin, *O Vospitanii Kommunistichesko*, soznatel'nosti Moscow, 1946.

V. Klemperer, *Die unbewältige Sprache*, Darnstadt, 1956.

Leszek Kolakowski, *L'Esprit révolutionnaire*, Brussels, Éd. Complexe. 1978.

A. Koyré, *Études sur l'histoire de la pensée philosophique en Russie*, Paris, 1950.

V. P. Krutous, 'O melodramaticheskom' in: *Voprosy filosofii*, no. 6, 1981.

Dominique Labbé, *Le Discours communiste*, Paris, 1977.
I. I. Levin, 'O semiotike iskazhenija istiny' in: *Informatsionnyje voprosy semiotiki, lingvistiki i avtomaticheskogo perevoda*, Vypusk, 4, Moscow, 1974.
E. Limonov, *Le Poète russe préfère les grands nègres*, Paris, 1980.
Andrzej Luczaj, 'Zniewolony jezyk' in: *Kultura*, 2, 1980, pp. 100-106.

N. J. Marr, *Jazyk i Myshlenie*, Letchworth, Herts, 1977.
Marsai (Du), *Traité des tropes*, Paris, 1977.
L Martinez, 'La Langue de bois soviétique' in: *Commentair*, winter 1982-1983, vol. 4, no. 16, pp. 506-515.
K. Marx, F. Engels, *The German Ideology*.
V. Maximov, *Saga o nosorogakh*, (*The Saga of the Rhinoceros*), Frankfurt-am-Main, 1981.
H. Moser, *Sprachliche Folgen der politischen Teilung Deutschlands*, Düsseldorf, 1962.

E. Neizvestnyj, '*Lik-Litso-Lichina*' in: *Kontinent*, no. 27, 1981
V. Nekrasov, *Les Carnet d'un badaud*, Paris, 1976.

G. Orwell, *1984*, London, 1949.
G. Orwell, *The Collected Essays, Journalism and Letters*, London, 1970.

J. Pasqualini (Bao Ruo-wang), *Prisoner of Mao*, London, 1975.
Theodor Pelster, *Die politische Rede im Westen und Osten Deutschlands*, Düsseldorf, 1966.
S. Piatetskaia, *Lire les journaux russes*, Moscow, 1975.

W. Pisarek, *Retoryka Dziennikarska*, Kraków, 1975.

G. Planty-Bonjour, *Hegel et la pensée philosophique en Russie*, The Hague, 1974.

Plato, *Sophist*.

A. Platonov, 'Sokrovennyj Chelovek', in: *Techenie Vremeni*, Moscow, 1971.

A. Platonov, *Chevengur*, Paris, 1972.

A. Platonov, *La Fouille*, Lausanne, 1974.

A. M. Pridanceva, *Mladshim shkolnikam o konstitutsii S.S.S.R.*, Mosocw, 1980.

O. Reboul, *Le Slogan*, Brussels, 1975.

O. Reboul, *Langage et idéologie*, Paris.

E. G. Riemschneider, *Veränderungen des deutschen Sprachen in der sowjetisch besetzten Zone Deutschlands seit 1945*, Düsseldorf, 1963.

M. Robespierre, *Oeuvres*, Paris, 1866.

Otto B. Roegele, 'Die Spaltung der Sprache' in: *Die politische Meinung*, Vol 36, May 1959.

V. S. Rogovin, 'Rost narodnogo blagosostojanija i problemy sovershenstvovanija raspredelitelikh otnoshenij' in: *Voprosy filosofii*, no. 6, 1981.

L. Rzevskij, *Jazyk i totalitarizm*, München, 1951.

A. M. Selishchev, *Jazyk revoljutsionnoj epokhi*, Moscow, 1928.

Patrick Seriot, 'L. I. Brezhnev et le discours sur la science' in: *Essais sur le discours soviétique*, Université de Grenoble III, 1981, pp. 7-63.

Patrick Seriot, 'Langue et idéologie dans le dictionnaire Oshego' in: *L'Enseignement du russe*, no. 23 (January 1977).

D. Shturman, *Myertvye khvatajut shyvykh, Citaja Lenina, Bukharina, Trotskogo*, London 1982.

A. Sleptsov, 'Pedagogicheskie Besedy' in: *Sovremennik*, vol. XCIV, 1863.
A. Solzhenitsyn, *The Gulag Archipelago*, London, 1974.
J. Stalin, *Marksizm i voprosy jazykosnanija*, Berlin, 1962.
J. Stalin, *The Principles of Leninism*, Peking, 1969.
N. V. Stankevich, *Perepiska*, Moscow, 1914.

L. L. Thomas, *The Linguistic Theories of N. Marr*, Berkeley, 1957.
V. Trostinikov, 'Konets epokhi samougozhdenija' in: *Kontinent*, no. 25.

Paul Valéry, *Cahiers I*, Paris, Gallimard, 1973.
A. G. Vishnevskij, 'Demograficheskoe otnoshenie i obshchevstvo' in: *Voprosy filosofii*, no. 4, 1981.
Voltaire, *Les plus belles lettres*, Paris, 1961.

G. Wagner, 'Die Leitartikel der *Pravda*: eine Textwissenschaftliche Analyse' in: *Festschrift für Heinz Wissemann*, Frankfurt a. M./Bern, 1977.
A. Walicki, *A History of Russian Thought from the Enlightenment to Marxism*, Stanford, 1979.
G. Walter, *La Conjuration du Neuf Thermidor*, Paris, 1974.
A. Wat, 'Semantyka jezyka stalinskiego' in: *Aneks*, 21, 1979, pp. 56-70.

A. Zinoviev, *Yawning Heights*, Lausanne, 1976.
M. Zoshchenko, 'Agitator' in: *Izbrannoe*, Leningrad, 1978, pp. 84-85.